MESSERSCHMITT

By the same author:
The U 12 Flamingo (Aircraft Profiles No. 257)

MESSERSCHMITT

Armand van Ishoven

OMEGA

GALLEON

First published in Great Britain in 1975
by Gentry Books Limited

First Galleon/Omega edition published in 1975
by Gentry Books Limited
15 Tooks Court, London EC4 A1LA

ISBN 0 9044 42047

Printed by Tinling (1973) Limited
Prescot, Merseyside

Contents

To Hilde

Foreword

The history of aviation, that unique adventure for mankind, is composed of a myriad interwoven life-stories. One of those most closely connected with aviation is the story of Willy Messerschmitt, one of the earliest gliding pioneers who was to become a professor, a designer of world-wide repute, and the head of one of the largest aerospace industries.

The name Messerschmitt has meant many different things to different people, ranging from the NSFK pilot's exhilaration while aerobatting an M 35 in a limpid sky on a sunny day in Bavaria, to the stark terror of the Belgian soldier seeking refuge in a roadside ditch from a machine-gunning ground-strafing Luftwaffe Bf 110 on 10th May 1940.

This book by no means claims to be a complete biography of Professor Messerschmitt. My objective has been to look into the career of this world-renowned aviation specialist and to highlight the most significant achievements in his long and varied contribution to the advance of the science of aeronautics, up to the time of Germany's collapse in 1945.

I could not have written this book without the kind help of many institutions and individuals, most of whom I consider as friends. I would like to express my gratitude to at least some of them: R. Bateson, C. Cains, E. Delbaere, F. Haubner, C. Hirth, R. Kokothaki, F. Kovacs, A. Maes, A. Mühlbacher, H. Obert, W. Radinger, R. Rombaut, O. Rumler, H. Schliephaker, K. Schnittke, P. Skogsted, H. Thiele, A. Tilbury, J. Underwood, G. Van Acker and O. Von Römer. Also the Abteilung der Militärflugplätze, Dübendorf; Bundesarchiv, Koblenz; Deutsches Museum, München; Flight International, London; Imperial War Museum, London; Lufthansa, Köln; Messerschmitt-Bölkow-Blohm GmbH, Ottobrunn; Stadtarchiv, Düsseldorf; US Navy, Washington; US Air Force, Washington; and VFW-Fokker, Hamburg.

Armand van Ishoven, September 1974

Note: Unless otherwise stated, all photographs are from the author's archives.

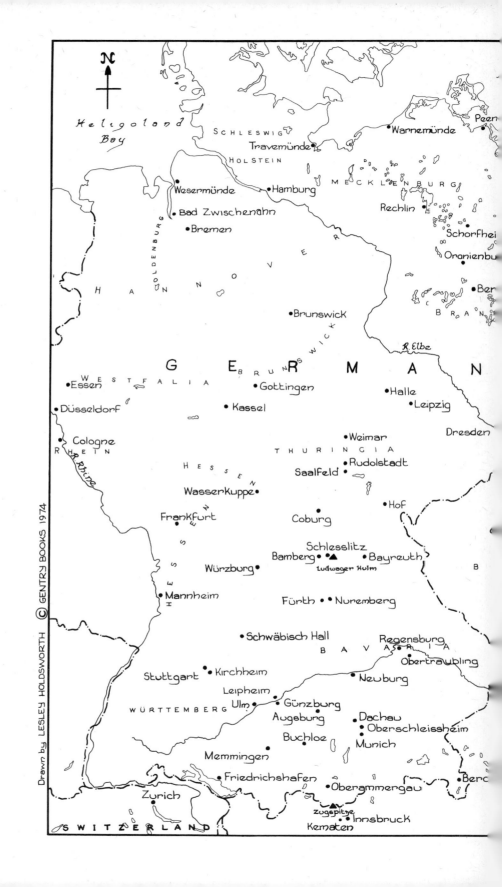

N

Heligoland Bay

SCHLESWIG
• Travemünde • Warnemünde Peen

HOLSTEIN

MECKLENBURG

• Wesermünde • Hamburg Rechlin
• Bad Zwischenahn Schorfhei
OLDENBURG
• Bremen • Oranienbu

H A N N O V E R • Ber

R

BRA N

• Brunswick

R. Elbe

G E B R U N S W I C K R M A N

WESTFALIA
• Essen • Gottingen • Halle
• Düsseldorf • Kassel • Leipzig

RHEIN • Weimar Dresden

Rhine • Cologne THURINGIA
H E S S E N • Rudolstadt
Saalfeld •
• Wasserkuppe •
• Hof
• Frankfurt • Coburg
H E S S E N
Schlesslitz
Bamberg • ▲ • Bayreuth
• Würzburg Ludwager Kulm B
• Mannheim
Fürth • Nuremberg

• Schwäbisch Hall Regensburg
B A V A R I A
Kirchheim • Obertraubling
Stuttgart •
Leipheim • Neuburg
Ulm • Günzburg
WÜRTTEMBERG Augsburg • Dachau
• Oberschleissheim
Buchloe • • Munich
Memmingen
• Friedrichshafen Berc
• Obergmmergau
Zurich ▲
Zugspitze • Innsbruck
S W I T Z E R L A N D Kematen

Drawn by LESLEY HOLDSWORTH © GENTRY BOOKS 1974

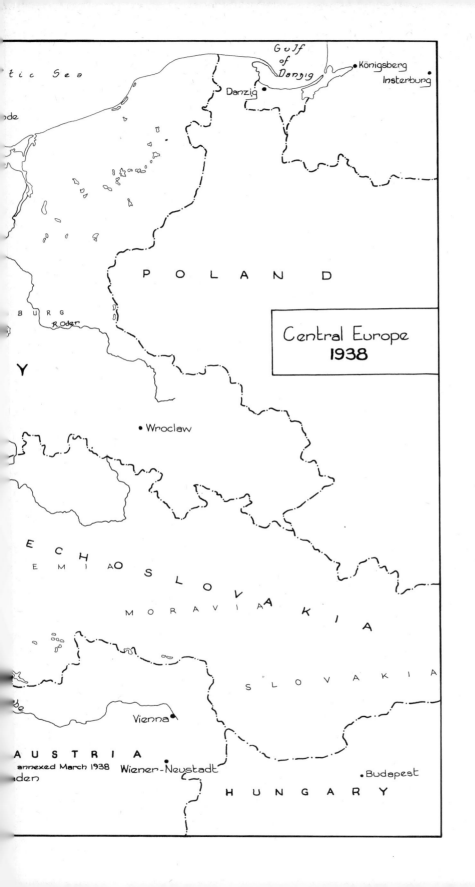

Central Europe
1938

Glossary

(Note: This is a selective rather than an exhaustive collection of German-language terms. Company status is defined by various ending abbreviations including AG, GmbH, and KG)

a.D.: (ausser Dienst). Literally 'out of Service'; retired serving officer

Abteilung Luftfahrt: Aviation Department of RVM (which see)

Akaflieg: (Akademische Fliegergruppe). Students' flying group or club

Bay-er, -erisch, -ern: Bavarian, Bavaria

Bf: (see BFW). Messerschmitt aircraft prefix, 1934–38; but retained in official handbooks, 1939–45, for such types as Bf 109 and Bf 110. (See also 'M', 'Me' and 'S')

BFW: (Bayerische Flugzeugwerke AG). Bavarian Aircraft Works; established in 1926 to take over Udet-Flugzeugbau GmbH and merged in 1927 with Messerschmitt-Flugzeugbau GmbH (Messerschmitt Aircraft Construction Co. Ltd)

Brigadeführer: (SS rank). Brigade commander

c/n: Manufacturer's individual aircraft construction or work's number. (See also 'W.Nr.')

DELA: (Deutsche Luftsport-Ausstellung). National sports-flying exhibition; in 1932, Berlin was venue

DFS: (Deutsche Forschungs Institut für Segelflug). State Institute for Glider Research

Dipl.Ing.: (Diplom-Ingenieur). Licensed or certificated engineer

DLH: (Deutsche Luft Hansa). State airlines

DLV: (Originally Deutscher Luftfahrt-Verband eV and later Deutscher Luftsport-Verband eV). DLV (1902–33) was the traditional, non-political national federation of independent flying clubs; politically superseded by the second DLV (1933–37) – the 'Air-Sport Union or Association' – which in turn gave way to the Nazi Party's overt NSFK or Fliegerkorps paramilitary movement in 1937

Dr. Ing.: (Doktor der Ingenieurwissenschaft). Doctor of Engineering

DVS: (Deutsche Verkehrsfliegerschule GmbH). National Transport Pilots' School; established Berlin-Staaken in 1925 and expanded to include (1927) among others an offshoot at Munich-Schleissheim

eV: (eingetragener Verein). Registered association

Flugkapitän: Flight-captain

Flugzeugbau: Aircraft construction enterprise. (See 'BFW')

Gauleiter: (Political rank). Administrator of a Gau, the main territorial unit of the NSDAP, Germany being divided into 42 Gaue

Generalfeldmarschall: Next to the specially-created 'Reichsmarschall' title for the Luftwaffe's commander-in-chief, Hermann Göring, this was highest field rank; RAF and USAF equivalents, Marshal of the Royal Air Force and General of the Air Force (5-star)

Generalleutnant: (RAF) Air Vice-Marshal; (USAF) Major-General (2-star)

Generalmajor: (RAF) Air Commodore; (USAF) Brigadier-General (1-star)

Generaloberst: (RAF) Air Chief Marshal; (USAF) General (4-star)

General der Flieger: (RAF) Air Marshal; (USAF) Lieutenant-General (3-star)

Generalluftzeugmeister: Director-General of (Luftwaffe) Equipment

Geschwader: Air force group. The Luftwaffe's largest formation, comprising approximately 100 aircraft, usually confined to one role

Gruppe: Air force wing

Hauptmann: (RAF) Flight-Lieutenant; (USAF) Captain

Jagdverband (JV): A formation of fighters; also General Galland's élite Me 262 fighter unit, JV 44 (1945)

JG: (Jagdgeschwader). Air force fighter group

Jäger: Literally 'hunter'; a fighter-category aircraft; also, a fighter pilot

Jägerstab: Inter-ministerial fighter-staff for increasing fighter production

Konstruktionsbüro: Construction design department

Kommissar: Inspector-General

Luftflotte: Air-fleet or (USAF) air force

Luftwaffe: German Air Force

M: Messerschmitt aircraft prefix (1924–34)

Me: Messerschmitt aircraft prefix superseding 'Bf' (which see)

Ministerialrat: Senior civil servant

NSDAP: (Nationalsozialistische Deutsche Arbeiter Partei). The National Socialist German Worker's Party or Nazi Party

Nordbayerische Verkehrsflug GmbH: North Bavarian Air Services founded in 1926 by Theo Croneiss

Obergruppenführer: (SS rank) Senior group leader

Oberleutnant: (RAF) Flying-Officer; (USAF) First-Lieutenant

Oberst: (RAF) Group-Captain; (USAF) Colonel

Projektbüro: Project design department

Regierungsbaumeister: Building and construction state overseer

Reich: The German State or Empire

Reichsleiter: (Political rank). State administrator

Reichsmarschall: Created for Göring when C-in-C Luftwaffe (see General-feldmarschall)

Reichspostminister: Postmaster-General

Reichstag: State parliament

Reichswehr: State Armed Forces, Navy and Army (1919–35)

RLM: (Reichsluftfahrtministerium). German Air Ministry (1933–45)

RM: (Reichsmark). Pre-Second World War basic unit of currency – now DM or Deutsche Mark – and readers who wish to make their own conversions of amounts quoted in the author's text may care to use the following 1974 equivalents (approximations):

	100 RM equals . . .	
1926	88p	US$2.11
1930	80p	$1.92
1935	£1.22	$2.93
1939	£1.40	$3.36

RVM: (Reichsverkehrsministerium). German Ministry of Transport

Staffel: Air force squadron

Staffelkapitän: Air Force officer commanding a squadron

S: (Segelflugzeug). Sailplane or glider; also Messerschmitt aircraft prefix (1912–1924) until replaced by 'M' (which see)

Technisches Amt: Technical Office of RLM

TG: (Transportgeschwader). Air force transport group

W.Nr.: (Werke Nummer). Manufacturer's individual aircraft work's or construction number. (See also 'c/n')

ZG: (Zerstörergeschwader). Literally 'Destroyer' and applied to bomber-escort, heavy-fighters including the Bf 110; thus, ZG is Heavy-Fighter Group

1
Gliding Apprenticeship

For all the world like some monstrous white winged insect, the frail contraption glided falteringly away from the slope of the hill. Suspended beneath the makeshift contrivance, working hard to keep its slow progress on an even keel, was its designer and builder – a 33-year-old architect named Friedrich Harth. In a matter of seconds, this pioneer German glider pilot had made landfall at the foot of the hill, the Ludwager Kulm. On this sunny day in 1913, Harth and his young helper, Willy Messerschmitt, had come to the hill, near Schlesslitz, from their home town of Bamberg, some ten miles to the west, to experiment further with their own hand-built glider.

Some of the inhabitants of Bamberg, a textile town which was founded in 804 AD by Saxon colonists and situated in the Kingdom of Bavaria, part of the German Reich, looked upon the two as an oddly assorted couple. Willy Emil Messerschmitt was now only 15 years old, and architect Harth was more than twice his age. Messerschmitt was born in Frankfurt am Main on 26th June 1898, the son of Ferdinand Messerschmitt, a wine merchant, and his wife Maria, née Schaller. He started going to school at the Frankfurt Adlerflychtschule in 1905, but the next year his family moved to Bamberg. Here he attended the Volksschule (primary school), spent two years at the Gymnasium (grammar school) and then went to the Realschule, a secondary school with a scientific bias. He was fascinated by the rapidly developing world of aviation ever since the time he first saw a Zeppelin, the *Bodensee*, in Friedrichshafen on Lake Constance. His enthusiasm grew after he visited the Internationale Luftfahrt-Ausstellung, the international aviation exhibition held in Frankfurt in 1909, and at the age of

Lanky young teenager Willy Messerschmitt listens attentively to last-minute launching instructions from his friend and fellow enthusiast, architect Friedrich Harth who is seated in his pioneer German 'canard' or tail-first glider, the S 1

12 he started building his first rubber-powered (elastic strand) model aircraft.

Friedrich Harth was born in Zentbeckhofen, near Bamberg, on 6th October 1880. Following Otto Lilienthal, he was the second to carry out experiments with gliders in Germany. A keen admirer of the Wright brothers, he had started experimenting in 1908 and had already made many an attempt to fly, first at Würzburg and later at Bamberg. In 1910 he started building a glider of his own design, which he called the S 1. This was of the 'canard' or tail-first type, having its tailplane in front of the wing rather than behind as in more conventional types to come. Its low weight made the S 1 simple to launch – in fact, one helper could tow it into the air by running down a slope – but its 'steering system' or flying controls hardly worked at all. Needless to say, the S 1 failed to come up to Harth's expectations.

In the meantime, Harth had made the acquaintance of young Willy Messerschmitt. Not surprisingly, the boy was only too happy to help with the experiments, and was himself soon making flights of up to 100 metres (300 feet). At this stage, Harth decided to build a new glider – called the S 4 – which was to be controlled by two 'joy-sticks' – a lateral control system favoured by the Wrights. The control column on the pilot's left-hand side warped the port or left wing, while that on the right-hand side warped the starboard or right wing. If both sticks were moved in the same direction they worked like a normal elevator, but if moved in opposite directions they acted as ailerons. The rudder bar operated normally. Messerschmitt's help in building and experimenting with this new type was both efficient and enthusiastic.

Airborne! Running down the slope of the Ludwager Kulm, in Bavaria, Willy Messerschmitt launches Harth in the S 1 glider. The relatively light construction permitted one-man launching. It was in this primitive glider that Messerschmitt had his first experiences of flying

In time, they realized that their original launching site on the Ludwager Kulm no longer provided sufficient room for their experiments and so moved to the Rhön Mountains. Here they found a suitable sloping terrain on the Heidelstein, near the Wasserkuppe where some Darmstadt students had started experimenting with gliders in 1911, and from where the German – and in fact world – gliding movement was to evolve and spread out after the First World War. They started by building a wooden shed, but they had hardly finished it when war broke out and Harth was mobilized into the Imperial Army. So that the work could continue, Harth handed the S 4 blueprints over to Messerschmitt, who was now a student at the Oberrealschule (secondary school) in Nuremburg.

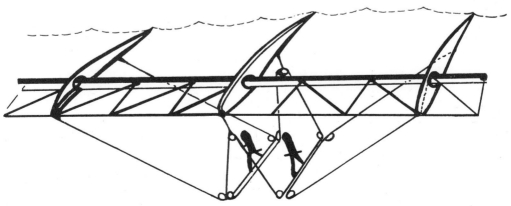

The wing-warping steering system used by Harth

At the end of the first war winter of 1914–15, Messerschmitt intended to start working alone in their Heidelstein shed, but when he arrived the following May he found to his disgust that it had been plundered by vandals. Undaunted, he set to work on their next project, the S 5, following sketches sent to him by Harth and making use of some parts of the S 4. His workshop was a room of his parents' restaurant-cum-wine-business.

When in 1915, Harth returned to Bamberg on leave, he was taken by surprise and astonished when Messerschmitt showed him the glider – completely finished. Without delay Harth undertook its first flight on the Heidelstein. Afterwards, he quickly drew up a new design incorporating various modifications suggested by this experience. Once again it was Messerschmitt who built this improved glider, the S 6. Later, in the year 1916, Harth was able to make a flight lasting three and a half minutes, at that time a formidable accomplishment. The monoplane was now already showing some resemblance to the

The First World War had run one year when this peaceful photograph was taken on the Heidelstein, in the Rhön mountains, in the autumn of 1915. Behind the 17-year old Messerschmitt (left) and Harth is the S 5 glider which owed its detail design and construction entirely to Willy Messerschmitt

The S 6 was essentially an improved version of the S 5 and was also tested in 1916 on the Heidelstein where this photograph was taken with designer-constructor Willy Messerschmitt seated at the controls

primary training gliders of the 1930s.

In the meantime, Harth had been transferred to the Flieger-Ersatz-Abteilung, the military flying school, at Schleissheim near Munich, where he instructed in the art of covering aircraft with linen and construction in general. At the end of 1916 he was joined by Messerschmitt who, after a short stay at a Minenwerfer-Einheit, a mortar instruction unit, was sent to serve at Schleissheim as well. They spent their off-duty hours experimenting with different wing sections and control systems.

After the war, Harth returned to his drawing board as an architect, and on

The S 6's lightness of construction coupled with the high-lift aerofoil potential is demonstrated as the port or left half of the mainplane is swung in a clockwise direction on the Heidelstein

Photo: Messerschmitt AG

At the age of 22 years, and a student at Munich's Technische Hochschule, Willy Messerschmitt already shows the mature bearing of the man of purpose he was destined to become

4th December 1918, patented his (S 4) flying control system using wing-warping by two 'joy-sticks' instead of ailerons. Messerschmitt, who had been given his military discharge on medical grounds in 1917, went to Munich to study at the Technische Hochschule, or technical college. Whenever free time, such as holidays, became available, Harth and Messerschmitt were to be found working on the Heidelstein; Messerschmitt not only participated actively in experimenting and building but to a large extent financed these undertakings.

During the period immediately following the war, gliding in Germany was brought to life through the efforts of the dedicated Oscar Ursinus, famous editor of *Flugsport*, the leading German magazine devoted to the sport of flying. Through his magazine, he called all gliding enthusiasts together for a contest on the Wasserkuppe, held from 15th July to 15th September 1920. This was the first of the annual Wasserkuppe contests, which were to become the top gliding event in Germany during the period between the two world wars. Throughout the first contest, however, Harth and Messerschmitt kept aloof on 'their' Heidelstein, telling no-one of their work.

At last, the time came when they decided that their results had achieved some value and they contributed an article to *Flugsport*, describing their work. This attracted the attention of the glider pilots at the Wasserkuppe. But, when a group of them decided to visit Harth and Messerschmitt they found only a locked shack, as the two men had left a few days before.

In the course of 1919 they built – this time in Munich – the Harth-Messerschmitt S 7 which they were able to try out in the same year on the Heidelstein, and which was to be improved upon and rebuilt many times in the years to come. In 1921 they founded a flying-school on the Heidelstein, which they advertised in *Flugsport*. Gliding at this time was still a very primitive and unorganized business. Gliding pilots were either ex-military pilots or people who had never flown at all, and who often tried to learn all by themselves. They were mostly of limited financial means and thus rarely paid any fee for flying tuition.

Now and then, the glider pilots gathered on the Wasserkuppe observed a moving object in the distance. It was the S 8, Harth's and Messerschmitt's newest project. Harth's ambition was to better the existing glider duration record. Orville Wright's 11-minute hitherto unchallenged record of 1910 had been improved by two minutes on 30th August 1921 by Klemperer, flying on the Wasserkuppe, only to be beaten a few days later by Martens, who on 5th September achieved a flight of 15 minutes. Harth hoped to be able to stay in the air for more than an hour, and was impatiently waiting for the right weather conditions. As predicted by the weather forecasters, a powerful south-westerly started to blow on 13th September and Harth prepared himself for his attempt on the record. He had to run only a few paces against the wind before he became airborne and soared into the air. As the wind was blowing at between 25 and 45 mph, he could easily stay at a hundred feet, now and then attaining more than 200 feet above the ground. The gale allowed him to remain above his launching point for minutes at a time and even to fly to and fro, towards the east as far as the Jungviehweide cattle meadow, and towards the west as far as the road to Bischofsheim. Messerschmitt and a helper watched Harth's flight with great excitement, and when it had lasted over a quarter of an hour, Messerschmitt rushed away to fetch a camera. As he did so, suddenly, Harth crashed from about 200 feet, probably as a result of a break in the control system. With serious fractures of the skull and pelvis, the unconscious Harth was carried away, never to recover completely.

The entire flight had lasted for 21 minutes. It was a world record, but could not be homologated for lack of official evidence.

While Harth recovered – he had to stay in hospital until 22nd March 1922 – Messerschmitt kept on building and making improvements to Harth's designs. Not all of these had Harth's approval, however, as is witnessed by a letter he

Disconsolately, Messerschmitt (left) gazes at the wreck of the S 8 on the Wasserkuppe, in the Rhön mountains, on 13th September 1921. Friedrich Harth had been at the controls creating an unofficial gliding record flight of 21 minutes before some constructional failure occurred. Harth escaped with his life but sustained serious injuries which kept him in hospital for six months

wrote to his brother Louis Harth, in which he said that he did not consider some of Messerschmitt's alterations to be improvements. Besides constructing the S 9, an unsuccessful flying-wing or tailless glider, Messerschmitt also experimented with various wing profiles. In the September issue of the *Zeitschrift für Flugtechnik und Motorluftschiffahrt*, a technical publication on the science of aeronautics, Messerschmitt published an article describing Harth's duration flight.

Finally the two decided to transfer their activities to the Wasserkuppe. Their first endeavour was to build a small wooden workshop which quickly became a refuge for many glider-pilots on misty days or stormy nights. Walter Georgii, later to become world-famous as a gliding meteorologist, related how the carpenter employed by Messerschmitt was equally good at making coffee or preparing a strong punch as at glueing wood. As Messerschmitt's was the only waterproof shed in the area, at times the whole gliding crowd could be found gathered there, especially on wet days.

Georgii also relates how, even then, one could recognize Messerschmitt's daring and brilliant style of aircraft design; their strength especially caused many a headache to the technical control commission, the examining body that had to approve every glider before it was allowed to be flown. Notwithstanding their progressive construction, however, Messerschmitt's designs withstood all aerodynamic loads.

On the Wasserkuppe, Messerschmitt became acquainted with many people who would one day become famous names in the German aviation industry. Among these were Hentzen, the glider pilot who in August 1922 broke the world duration and height record on the Wasserkuppe, and Blume who later

The S 10 was a logical progression in the line of Harth-Messerschmitt high-wing monoplane gliders and had a claim to fame in that it was intended to be the first design to be put into limited production. In the same year, 1922, Wolf Hirth (seen here) learned to fly on the S 10

rose to fame as the designer of the Arado line of aircraft. When Blume was about to make his first flight, and was already seated in the glider, he calmly announced: 'Gentlemen, will you explain to me once and for all what I have to do? After all, I have never sat in such a contraption before.'

In 1922, Messerschmitt and Harth at last succeeded in establishing their flying school. Their first pupil was Wolf Hirth, who had learned to fly with an S 10. Together with Paul Brenner, Wolf Hirth had already entered the first Rhön contest in 1920; their biplane glider was built by the Flugtechnischer Verein Stuttgart and had been given the last competition number, '26'. When he had more-or-less learned to fly, Hirth joined the Harth-Messerschmitt 'firm'. This simply meant that he started building a few S 10s together with an unemployed sculptor in the back room of a small inn at Bischofsheim, rented by Messerschmitt, who had returned to study at his furnished room on the Odeonsplatz in Munich. Later, the whole 'business' was transferred to a workshop on the outskirts of Munich.

By the time the third Rhön contest began, they had completed two S 10s. Unfortunately, the first time Wolf Hirth took one of these into the air, he crashed, injuring his larynx so seriously that his voice was never normal again. These Rhön contests cannot be compared to present-day gliding contests, and may be described more accurately as 'camps'. Enthusiasts simply gathered for some flying and in the hope of winning some of the prizes, although no daily tasks were set. During the first two weeks of the 1922 contest, no special flights were made; gliders were tested and pilots learnt to fly by performing short hops. It was during this 'warming-up' period that Wolf Hirth crashed.

Friedrich Harth made a few flights in the new S 11, but he was becoming less and less interested in aviation. In 1923 he lost his job as a schoolmaster and remained unemployed until 1933, when he was appointed Oberbaurat, or consultant engineer, in Bamberg. He and Messerschmitt remained on friendly terms all the time they worked together, even though they had many arguments over technical details. Messerschmitt was always pushing forward the more progressive solution, while being held back by the more cautious and systematic Harth. Even at this time, Messerschmitt was a staunch advocate of ultra-light construction, which he will remain forever. In 1923 Messerschmitt decided to go his own way and founded his own enterprise in Bamberg, the Flugzeugbau

Yet another variation of open-framework design, the S 13 is being hauled up a Rhön slope in 1922 by 'cow-power'. For the local peasants, the gliders provided occasional and welcome additional revenue

For the next design, the S 14, Messerschmitt's bold decision to produce an enclosed, wooden fuselage glider was rewarded at the 1923 Rhön Contest; the S 14 gained first prize for best altitude attained

Messerschmitt, undeterred by the fact that he was still a student and only twenty-five years old.

With the help of Wolf Hirth he built in his father's establishment, the restaurant at the Schönleinsplatz, a high-wing monoplane glider with a covered wooden fuselage – the S 14. Hirth, who in the meantime had taken over the day-to-day management of the flying school, test-flew the new glider, but he crashed from a height of some 60 feet and fractured his pelvic bone. The quest for structural lightness and the inexperience of most pilots was the reason why so many of these early gliders crashed, and in fact no fewer than three S 12s crashed one after the other.

The second S 14 to be built by Messerschmitt was to permit the pilot Hackmack to attain the greatest altitude during the Rhön contest of 1923. Messerschmitt received the prize money for building the most successful glider of the meet, and used the prize money to build his next two designs, the S 15 and the S 16.

The finances of the newly founded Flugzeugbau Messerschmitt were rather limited, as is evidenced by the highly unorthodox 'throwing organization' introduced by Hirth. Only a limited number of tools was available and these had to be used in turn by the manager – Hirth – and his three helpers. Much time was lost in passing the few tools to each other and so they practised throwing them – hammers, chisels, pincers, and other dangerous projectiles. Needless to say, the system was soon abandoned.

The S 14 was not just a financial success for Messerschmitt. After an initial refusal, he was allowed to use the design as his thesis at the final examination before receiving his title of Diplom-Ingenieur, or certified engineer, instead of the prescribed 'Design of a Crane'. It was the first time such a thing had happened at the technical college although the practice would later on become commonplace in Germany, as many students of the Akademische Fliegergruppen, the college flying clubs, designed gliders for their theses.

Messerschmitt had now parted company with his original partner, Friedrich Harth, and had come to the conclusion that the control method developed by his old friend was not the right solution, and also that powered aircraft afforded far more possibilities than gliders. The construction of powered aircraft had been forbidden in Germany by the Treaty of Versailles, but after May 1922 it was again allowed even though many restrictions were still imposed. For example, a single-seater with an engine of more than 60 hp was considered to be a military aircraft and thus forbidden, likewise any aircraft that could be flown without a pilot or that was equipped with armour or provision for armament, or with an engine supercharger. Maximum speed was restricted to 170 km/h (106 mph), maximum ceiling to 4,000 m (13,000 ft), maximum useful load, including pilot, mechanic and instruments, to 600 kg (1,300 lb). Maximum quantity of fuel and oil was limited by a formula which took into account the maximum speed. During the period leading up to 1922, gliding had played a vitally important role in German aviation, after the Treaty of Versailles had put so many obstacles in its way. But now, like so many other well-known personalities in German aviation, Messerschmitt turned from gliding to powered flying.

2
Becoming an Industrialist

Messerschmitt's next two designs were not yet fully fledged aircraft, but gliders with small engines. As his parental home was no longer big enough, he had to rent space at the Murrmann Brewery at Bamberg where, thanks to the financial help of his elder brother Ferdinand, he was able to employ five workers.

In this building at Bamberg, formerly used by the Murrmann Brewery, Flugzeugbau Messerschmitt was the starting point for powered-glider and powered-aircraft construction from 1923 to 1925

In developing from motorless-aircraft to powered-aircraft, Messerschmitt gained experience in 1924 by exploiting the basic concept of the S 14 and installing a British 14-hp Douglas (motor-cycle) engine; the result was the S 15. Unfortunately the power unit proved to be unsatisfactory for this powered-glider

The annual gliding contest at the Rhön gliding centre, already taking a very special place in German aviation, was scheduled to take place in the summer of 1924 for the fifth time. In order to stimulate the development of ultra-light powered aircraft or powered gliders, Oskar Ursinus, organizer and guiding light of the yearly contests, decided to hold a special contest for this class of aircraft. Messerschmitt decided to enter, and started experimenting with his S 15, equipped with a 14-hp Douglas (UK) motorcycle engine. His test pilot, Hauptmann a.D. Seywald, succeeded in making flights of up to 45 minutes' duration, attaining a height of 600 m (2,000 ft). In the contest, Messerschmitt entered two powered gliders: the S 16a *Bubi* and the S 16b *Betti*. *Bubi* was written off when it was destroyed during a forced-landing after losing its propeller; *Betti* also had to make an emergency landing because of a break in its

The S 16b – *Betti* – which Messerschmitt entered for the 1924 Rhön contest. It was powered by a 21-hp Douglas (motorcycle) engine

drive chain. The contest was won by Ernst Udet – the second greatest fighter 'ace' of the First World War – flying his Kolibri (Hummingbird). Messerschmitt now realized that he clearly needed more experience with aeroengines. He received some orders from local Bavarian flying clubs and, as the rented space in the brewery proved too cramped for him to be able to fulfil them, he moved to a discarded ammunitions factory near Bamberg.

After the two powered gliders came Messerschmitt's first real aircraft, the M 17. From now on he no longer designated his types with an 'S' for Segelflugzeug (gliding/sailing aircraft) but with an 'M' for Messerschmitt. The M 17 was a small 2-seat high-wing all-wood monoplane with open cockpit. The single-spar wing construction Messerschmitt used on this type had previously been used on gliders only, and never before on an aircraft. It could be fitted with either a 24-hp ABC Scorpion (UK) or a 30-hp Bristol Cherub (UK). One of these aircraft was exhibited at the Munich Verkehrsausstellung, the transport exhibition. During 1925, Theo Croneiss – a First World War fighter pilot with five confirmed victories – entered the M 17 in several contests and was able to achieve good places in the Rundflug, the top annual sports flying event in Germany, and in the Oberfrankenflug, a sports flying event in Upper Franconia held from 2nd to 4th May. During this last contest, the M 17 reached a height of 1,350 m (4,430 ft) and proved to have a maximum speed of 150 km/h (93 mph) and a minimum speed of 65 km/h (40 mph). During the navigation trial, Croneiss became lost – even to the extent of straying into Czechoslovakia. In light of the good performance of the M 17, *Flugsport* did not stint its praise:

The first M-for-Messerschmitt designation was applied to the company's first powered-aircraft, the M 17, which did well in competitive events staged in 1925. Willy Messerschmitt poses with certain pride; the engine is a 30-hp Bristol Cherub

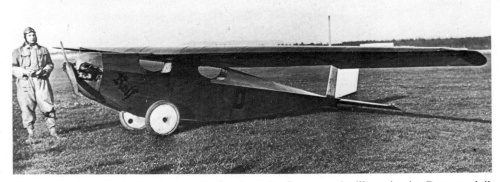

This M 17 photographed in 1926 is straight from the factory and still awaits the German civil registration although an individual name *Rolf* has been inscribed behind the Cherub engine. One of the feats undertaken by an M 17 was to cross the Alps in a flight from Bamberg to Rome by von Conta and von Langsdorf

'The success of this machine proves that a powered glider will become the aircraft of the future.' These contests earned Messerschmitt some 10,000 RM in prize money, which he used to enlarge his business.

In the autumn of 1926, Werner von Langsdorf, a former war-pilot and a member of the Akademische Fluggruppe Darmstadt, the students' flying club of Darmstadt, decided to participate in the top Italian annual aerosport event, the Coppa d'Italia. With his passenger von Conta, he flew their M 17 across the formidable Alps, from Bamberg to Rome; quite a feat for such a small and low-powered aircraft.

Two flying schools placed orders for a total of four machines, but in the commercial sense all these successes were of little importance. In the *Jahrbuch der bayerischen Wirtschaft 1926*, a Bavarian economic yearbook the text of which was completed in November 1925, Hans Herrmann wrote eight pages about Udet-Flugzeugbau, then one of the largest German aircraft manufacturers whose chief engineer was in fact Herrmann himself. But of Messerschmitt he wrote laconically: 'In Bavaria, besides Udet, Messerschmitt also builds motor gliders as a hobby.'

While the M 17 was being built, Messerschmitt had been visited by Theo Croneiss, who had become one of Germany's foremost sports pilots. He was at Bamberg to start a flying school and was already acquainted with Messerschmitt as they had met at the Wasserkuppe. While having supper one evening at the Messerschmitt restaurant, he witnessed a talk between Messerschmitt and a financier. Messerschmitt was in some financial difficulty at the time, and the financier tried to avail himself of this opportunity to get hold of some of his patents at a very low price. When the financier left the room for a moment,

Croneiss asked the nervous Messerschmitt how much money he needed. The cheque for 4,500 RM that Croneiss immediately handed over allowed Messerschmitt to turn away the financier and formed the beginning of a long partnership. On 28th April 1926, the two men founded the Messerschmitt Flugzeugbau GmbH, with a capital of 10,000 RM. Registered in Bamberg, the company had as its declared goal the design, construction and sale of aircraft and parts thereof, together with all aspects of commercial and sports aviation and air publicity.

On 6th January 1926, the numerous small German airlines still in existence had been merged into one, largely as a result of pressure exerted by Major a.D. Ernst Brandenburg, the director of the Abteilung Luftfahrt, the aviation section, of the Reichsverkehrsministerium (RVM), the German Ministry of Transport. The new company, Deutsche Luft Hansa (DLH) was placed under the directorship of Erhard Milch. Since DLH was subsidised by the German Government, Milch saw one of its primary tasks as aid to the German aircraft industry as a whole; in order that as many aircraft manufacturers as possible should benefit from this aid, he accepted as a necessary evil the fact that Luft Hansa's fleet would consist of many different types.

Despite the fact that Luft Hansa was now the only airline in Germany with the right to subsidies from the German Reich, barely two months later Theo Croneiss set up his own small airline. This was the Nordbayerische Verkehrsflug GmbH, founded at Bamberg on 25th March 1926. In conjunction with Messerschmitt Flugzeugbau GmbH, Croneiss raised the necessary capital of 50,000 RM to set up a network feeding the major airports served by Luft Hansa. The States of Bavaria and Thuringia, together with several city treasuries, guaranteed Nordbayerische a minimum revenue and so, on 26th July, the company was able to inaugurate its first service flight. This was flown over a circular route: Nuremburg/Fürth – Bamberg – Coburg – Rudolstadt – Saalfeld – Weimar – Halle – Leipzig – Hof – Bayreuth – Nuremburg/Fürth. Some of the towns served were separated by a distance of scarcely 30 km (18 miles)! In the same month, the limits placed upon aircraft construction in Germany were abolished. Only the construction of military aircraft remained forbidden.

Croneiss's successes with his M 17 prompted him to ask Messerschmitt to design a small airliner for Nordbayerische Verkehrsflug. He stipulated that it should be a four-seater and cost less than 25,000 RM. After he had placed a firm order for four machines of this type – which was designated the M 18 – the Bavarian Government gave Messerschmitt 20,000 RM towards its development. First he built a wooden prototype, but being unsuccessful in selling this Messerschmitt then turned resolutely to building metal aircraft. The wooden prototype and the first metal M 18 were equipped with a 96-hp Siemens (Ger.) engine. The pilot sat in an open cockpit and the fuselage offered room for three

The M 18 prototype. This was Messerschmitt's first airliner, seating four passengers, with deliveries starting in 1926. The passenger door, unusually, was on the starboard or right-hand side of the fuselage

passengers. The landing-gear axle ran along the underside of the fuselage.

The next four machines, of the M 18b type, had a 125-hp Siemens and carried four passengers. The M 18c was meant for aerial survey photography and possessed a wider, better sprung undercarriage. The next development was the M 18d for six passengers, offered with different engines ranging from 125-

Building the metal M 18 in 1927

Photo: BFW

Four passengers for the Deutsche Verkehrsflug (National Air Services) Düsseldorf–Cologne route having their photograph taken in front of an M 18d of 1930, sporting a more sophisticated landing gear than the M 18b. Note the departure and arrival panel, a practice borrowed from the railways. Aircraft illustrated has a Czechoslovak 150-hp Walter Mars engine. Passenger door now on the more conventional left-hand side of the fuselage

A proud businessman about to embark in an M 18b D-1405 (W.Nr. 370) of Nordbayerische Verkehrsflug for a flight from Düsseldorf to Cologne. The aircraft's individual name, on the rudder, is *Gera*. The biplane just visible is a U 12 Flamingo

to 240-hp, such as the Siemens Sh-12, the Walter Mars (Czechoslovak.), the Wright Whirlwind (US) and the Armstrong Siddeley Lynx (UK). A last version, with a 300-hp Wright Whirlwind, was equipped with twin floats, connected to the fuselage by no fewer than 14 struts.

A total of 25 M 18s was built. Of these, 2 went to Switzerland and 1 to Portugal. It proved to be a very economical commercial transport. One of the export aircraft went to the Swiss Ad Astra airline, costing 95,000 Swiss francs. At home, many were used with great success on the short routes of the Nord-bayerische Verkehrsflug GmbH. Every town in Germany sought to be connected to the network of airlines, and these occasions were often celebrated with great festivities. Such was the case on 25th July 1926, when an M 18 (Werk Nummer or construction number 27), civil registration D-947, was taken into service at the airport of the city of Fürth, equipped with a Siemens Sh-11 and owned by Nordbayerische Verkehrsflug GmbH. When one month later, on Sunday 29th August, Ernst Udet came to Fürth to give one of his splendidly thrilling flying displays, D-947 was used to give 'joy-rides' to the people of the city. At the end of 1926, Messerschmitt organized his own modest flying display, at which some thirty invited guests were given the opportunity of viewing Bamberg from the air.

In 1927, the Deutscher Luftfahrt-Verband eV. (DLV) organized a contest

Another M 18d (W.Nr. 476), this time powered by a British 225-hp Armstrong Siddeley Lynx radial. The Swiss-registered CH 191 was operated by the Ad Astra Aero airline, and later by Swissair when it was reregistered HB-IME

An M 18b, one of several purchased by Theo Croneiss for his airline, Nordbayerische Verkehrs-flug GmbH. On the rudder is D-1266's (W.Nr. 369) individual name, *Schweinfurt*

at Leipzig – the Sachsenflug – which was held from 30th August to 5th September. The DLV was Germany's traditional aviation federation of independent flying clubs, founded in 1902, and its events were followed with great
interest by all sports flyers. The handicapping system used in the Sachsenflug
gave many advantages to those aircraft that could carry a great weight (pay
load) in relation to their own weight. For this contest Messerschmitt designed
the M 19, a wooden-construction, low-wing single-seater, which received an
infinite handicap as the payload was higher than the empty weight. Two aircraft

An M 19, D-1206, getting the starter's flag in the 1927 Sachsenflug, with E. von Conta at the
controls. This contest was won by Theo Croneiss flying another M 19, registered D-1221

of this type took part in the contest which they had theoretically won before it began. Both aircraft were equipped with 30-hp Bristol Cherubs (UK), and they were piloted by von Conta and Croneiss, the latter winning the contest in M 19 registered D-1221 and earning Messerschmitt 60,000 RM in prize money. No fewer than six Klemm L 20s participated in this event, characteristic of the great success of Hans Klemm's designs in the field of light aircraft.

The many orders for the M 18 had presented Messerschmitt and Croneiss with a financial problem. They needed credit before they could start building the aircraft ordered, and so approached the Bavarian Government for a loan. At the same time, the Bavarian Government had received a demand for a loan from BFW[1], Bayerische Flugzeugwerke, an aircraft company from Augsburg which in June 1926 had arisen from Udet-Flugzeugbau. Since 1922, Udet-Flugzeugbau had been engaged in the development and construction of sports, training and transport aircraft, taking up large loans in the process from the banking house of Merck, Finck & Co. It had proved impossible to effect a healthy economic situation – especially after Udet and his engineer Scheuermann had left the company – and was faced with increasingly grave financial difficulties. The company had to rely upon Merck, Finck & Co, as well as the Bavarian State and the RVM for support, but even though the bank had invested some 800,000 RM towards the end of July 1926, no dividends were forthcoming. Negotiations with the RVM and the Bavarian State led to the formation of a new company, BFW, to take over the assets and liabilities of Udet-Flugzeugbau, which company was then dissolved. The new company was formed on 20th July 1926 by the German Reich, the Bavarian State and Merck, Finck & Co., its stock being worth 400,000 RM. The German Reich represented by the Reich's Minister of Transport subscribed 250,000 RM, the Bavarian State represented by the Bavarian Trade Ministry 100,000 RM and Merck, Finck & Co. 50,000 RM.

During the spring of 1926, Udet-Flugzeugbau had negotiated with Eisenwerk Gebrüder Frisch with a view to acquiring the factory of the former Rumplerwerke AG in Augsburg, as the Udet factory was situated at Ramersdorf, near Munich, where no airfield was available. In July a contract was drawn up but never signed. The newly founded BFW went through with this contract, however, so that all its equipment together with that of Udet-Flugzeugbau was moved to Augsburg in the beginning of August 1926. Udet's

---

[1] This BFW should not be confused with another firm of the same name, which had been founded in 1916 as a sub-company of the Albatros-Werke succeeding the Ottowerke. This company had only built aircraft under licence, and shortly after the 1918 Armistice had merged with BMW, Bayerische Motorenwerke.

chief engineer Hans Herrmann was retained but the manager, Mr Pohl, was dismissed as he was blamed for the financial ruin of the Udet company. Instead, the management was entrusted to Dr Alexander Schruffer. The man who was to become the commercial director, Rakan Kokothaki, joined the firm on 13th August 1926.

The company obtained a loan of 400,000 RM, in addition to the original investment from the RVM, at a yearly interest of 5 per cent, and so some of its former debts could now be paid back. However, the acquisition of real estate and buildings at Augsburg, the removal, improvements and repairs, together with the inevitable lack of any production for a certain period all cost a great deal; and so the situation at the share-holders' meeting on 10th January 1927 was anything but rosy. Fritz Hille, the new manager, succeeded in having the loan from the RVM changed into an outright gift, and this subsidy was increased by 90,000 RM on the condition that Merck, Finck & Co. was ousted from the company. Its shares of 50,000 RM were taken up by the RVM.

BFW planned to use its Augsburg plant for mass-production of the Flamingo, which had already been manufactured by Udet-Flugzeugbau. Situated in the hangars of the former Bayerische Rumplerwerke, this plant was described in *Flugsport* on 23rd November 1927. It was on the road to Haunstetten, near a railway station. The adjacent field, owned by the municipality, was rented for factory use. The workshops were very modern and were equipped with all

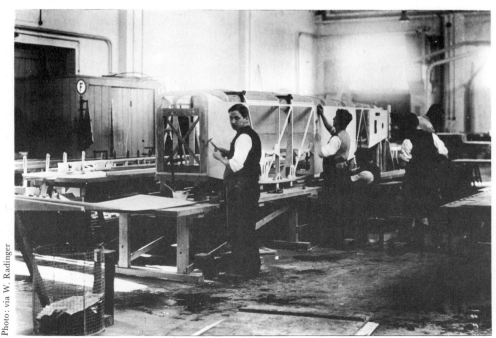

Photo: via W. Radinger

In the 1920s, aircraft construction was the work of real craftsmen in wood and metal. Flamingos being built by BFW at Augsburg in 1928

necessary machinery. For test-flying, a special hangar was available, together with a testing laboratory. The company's trademark, a stylised climbing eagle, was designed by a Munich artist, Alfred Zacharias. Udet's former engineer, Hans Herrmann, had many differences of opinion with the new management, leading to his departure in the autumn of 1926 when he went to work for the Caspar aircraft company at Travemünde.

So we see that BFW had adequate space for manufacturing, while Messerschmitt Flugzeugbau had insufficient facilities to fulfil an order for eight M 18s. Both companies were now applying to the Bavarian State for aid, but the unfavourable economic conditions of the time made support for them both out of the question. As a solution to the problem, it was proposed that any support should be dependent upon mutual co-operation between the two companies. This proposition was supported by the RVM and was placed before the parties concerned by their representative Major a.D. Ernst Brandenburg, the director of the Abteilung Luftfahrt of the RVM, and an ex-First World War pilot, who was to play a major role in building up a secret German air force.

As he had already met with some success, Messerschmitt was reluctant to sacrifice any control, at least as far as design and development were concerned. But after long and difficult negotiations, an agreement was finally reached in the autumn of 1927. It was agreed that BFW would give up design and development and concentrate on aircraft production; specifically those designed by Messerschmitt in the first instance. Messerschmitt Flugzeugbau would correspondingly limit its activities to developing new types, over which BFW would have priority of manufacture. Both firms would continue to exist as independent companies, and to that effect a contract was signed on 8th September 1927. Willy Messerschmitt now moved his personnel and equipment to Augsburg, where work was started at the end of 1927. A new engineer also joined the team, Dipl. Ing. Karl Theiss. The company's telegraphic address: Bayernflug. Poised as he was after the hectic year now drawing to a close, Messerschmitt was still a comparatively young man of just under 30 years of age.

3
Building in Quantity

Udet-Flugzeugbau had started building light sports aircraft back in 1922. The company had manufactured a very small series of the U 2, U 6 and U 10, together with a passenger transport, the U 8[1], a cantilever parasol monoplane four-seater, two of which were used by DLH. An ambitious four-motor eleven-seat transport high-wing monoplane was also built, the U 11 Kondor. This could eventually have been developed into a bomber, but it did not meet with success.

The U 12 or Flamingo[2] was the first biplane designed for the company by

---

[1] The U 8b version was the first German aircraft to be equipped with the British developed Handley Page-Lachmann wing slats – the ultimately famous 'Handley Page slots'. The slotted wing is a device that makes it possible for an aircraft to fly at a slower speed than is possible with a normal wing. On its leading edge is a small aerofoil that normally fits snugly against or into the main-wing section. This aerofoil is mounted on links or slides so that it can move forward, either automatically or manually, sending a current of air through the slot between the aerofoil and the wing. This straightens out the flow over the wing so that the wing retains its lift until a much greater angle-of-attack, and a lower forward speed, is reached. Messerschmitt first used the Handley Page slots on his M 27b, and later on his Bf 109.

[2] The U 12 Flamingo is treated exhaustively in the author's monograph on this type, published as No 257 in the *Aircraft Profiles* series. (Profile Publications Ltd, Windsor, England.)

Hans Herrmann. It was a two-seat biplane trainer and had been designed in the winter of 1924–5. It was to become one of the most popular trainers in Germany during the late 1920s. Before substantial orders had been received, however, Udet-Flugzeugbau had experienced severe financial difficulties and, as has been recorded already, was taken over by BFW in July 1926.

The first version, the U 12a, was equipped with an 80-hp Siemens engine,

A U 12 Flamingo under construction. Dual control is provided. The 'Augsburg Eagle' Messer-schmitt symbol is much in evidence

Photo: Messerschmitt-Bölkow-Blohm via O. Rumler

DVS Flamingos practising formation flying above the baroque Schloss (castle) Ober-Schleissheim next to the Schleissheim airfield, where one of the two most important DVS branches was based

Photo: Heinrich Dreyer

and a later version, the U 12b, with a 115-hp Siemens. The aircraft was eminently suited to aerobatics and became the standard trainer at the DVS, the Deutsche Verkehrsfliegerschule or German commercial flying school, at Schleissheim, near Munich. Ostensibly, the only pupils were airline pilots, but in fact a number of pilots for the underground German Air Force were trained in secret. Many officers who were to play an important role in the Luftwaffe learned to fly on a Flamingo.

The well-known German aviatrix, Thea Rasche, went to the USA with her personal Flamingo to take part in several air meets. On 12th August 1927, her birthday, she was forced to land in the Hudson River after the Siemens engine 'quit'. Especially famous was Udet's U-12 Spezial (c/n. 269, civil registration

Like Ernst Udet, Thea Rasche had her U 12 Flamingo (D-1120) fuselage painted red. In America, she was forced to make an emergency landing in the Hudson River on 12th August 1927 – she was on her way to her birthday party. She had given several aerobatic displays in the USA before this incident. The Flamingo was replaced by another U 12

Photo: Thea Rasche

Thea Rasche with another red fuselage aircraft: her M 23b, in 1931, shortly before experiencing elevator failure. The hangar in the background is that of Ernst Heinkel at Warnemünde

Ernst Udet standing before his red fuselage Flamingo (D-822). With him is Willy Stör, aerobatics instructor at the DVS in Schleissheim and demonstration pilot for BFW. The cine-cameraman could be assured of a hair-raising aerobatic display

D-822) with which he took part in a great many flying meets from 1925 to 1934, among others in September 1931 at Cleveland and in July 1933 at Los Angeles. One of the stunts he pioneered became particularly renowned, in which Udet lifted a handkerchief from the ground, or from the roof of a car for that matter, by means of a small stick fastened to his wingtip.

Altogether, some 150 Flamingos were built by BFW. Although military flying was forbidden in Austria and Hungary as well as in Germany, Flamingos

D-822 was Udet's personal Flamingo, which he used for his demonstrations at Cleveland in 1931 and at Los Angeles in 1932

Photo: Messerschmitt-Bölkow-Blohm

An attempt to improve on the Flamingo resulted in the BFW 1 Sperber (Sparrow-hawk) with a steel-tube frame fuselage and more conventional N-type steel-tube wing struts. Only this proto-type (D-1315) was built; it was evaluated by the DVS and was later owned by Alexander von Bismarck who flew it at air shows

were used in both countries for training military pilots in secret. Flamingos were licence-built in Riga, Latvia, by the Backman company, and in Budapest, Hungary, by the Weiss company. The Hungarians developed a special variant, the Hungaria, and the Austrians the U 12O, also referred to as the U 12S.

Before taking it into production, BFW had tried to improve the U 12 by replacing its wooden fuselage by a steel-tube type. To this end, the BFW I Sperber (Sparrow-hawk) and the BFW 3a Marabu (Stork), both designed by Karl Theiss, were built. They did not prove to be a success, however, and only one prototype of each was built.

Herrmann's last design for Udet-Flugzeugbau was the U 13 Bayern (Bavaria),

BFW aircraft on parade before the Augsburg works. The BFW 3a Marabu (Stork) is in the foreground, followed by a BFW 1 and seven Flamingos

a 450-hp biplane floatplane especially developed for the German Navy's
seaplane contest at Warnemünde in June 1926. The construction was taken
over by BFW but, because of propeller difficulties, it could not take part in the
contest for which it had been designed. It was lost later on while being tested by
BFW on the Starnberger See (Lake). Messerschmitt himself disliked biplanes.

In 1928 a storm was raised in the German Reichstag over the fact that the
Bavarian State owned shares in BFW, a factory that was capable eventually of
producing military aircraft. To avoid any further trouble, the Bavarian State
decided to sell its shares. Among those interested in purchasing them were
Ernst Heinkel of Warnemünde and Albatros of Berlin-Johannisthal. However,
the State only wanted to sell the shares at their full value, so no buyers could be
found initially. Meanwhile, Messerschmitt, fearing that he would lose his
independence, succeeded in persuading his friends in Bamberg, the Strohmeyer-
Raulino family, and especially Frau Lilly Strohmeyer née Michel-Raulino, to
take up the shares. On 1st July 1928, the total 400,000 RM shares were bought
at full value from the Bavarian State.

The new committee of shareholders was as follows: Herr Otto Strohmeyer
the chairman, from Bamberg; Prof. Dr Paul Rieppel; Dr V. Scancony, a
lawyer; and Dr Hellmann, Ministerialrat; the last three coming from Munich.
Dr Schruffer was replaced as manager by Fritz Hille and Willy Messerschmitt,
the latter owning 70,000 of the total of 400,000 RM of shares. The development
department of Messerschmitt Flugzeugbau GmbH was taken over by BFW
AG and the contract between the two firms now became void. This was never
formally carried out, however, and so Messerschmitt Flugzeugbau retained
ownership of all the Messerschmitt patents, a fact which was to be of great
importance later on.

By this time, Germany was badly hit by the Depression and many aircraft
factories were being forced to close down. BFW managed to survive by building
the M 18 and the U 12, and the M 18 in its turn, being extremely economical
to run, allowed the Nordbayerische Verkehrsflug to survive as the sole competitor to Luft Hansa.

When considering the construction of the M 18 and the M 19, the four main
characteristics of Messerschmitt's particular style of aircraft design become
apparent. They are: Simplicity of conception, minimal weight, minimal
aerodynamic drag and continual development. These characteristics will be
found in any aircraft designed by him or under his supervision.

Messerschmitt always tried to solve any design problem in the simplest way
possible. Thus he would use a thicker skin so as to be able to diminish the number
of stringers. Or, again, he would often use single forged- or cast-metal parts,
often of magnesium alloy, rather than parts built up of many separate pieces.

Sometimes Messerschmitt has obtained minimal weight by making one part

The first practical aero-tows. U 12 Flamingos were used to pioneer this novel method of launching gliders in the early 1930s

Drawing of a Flamingo equipped with a towing device, from the Hungarian aviation magazine *Aviatica*, 1932

The Flamingo D-1540 in 1931 at the Wasserkuppe gliding centre, where it was used for many years to tow gliders, piloted by Peter Riedel. Note the steel-tube array used to support the towing hook. The operator's name appears on the fin: Forschungsinstitut der RRG; Heimatflughafen (home base) Darmstadt

Cutaway drawings of the M 17, the M 18w (the float-equipped version) and the M 19 (from the
Messerschmitt Typenbuch, Graphischer Büro, Augsburg, Christmas 1943)

An aerial view of the BFW works at Augsburg in winter 1928. Line-up includes no fewer than 20 Flamingos and 5 Heinkel HD 17 military advanced-trainers

fulfil two functions. A typical example of this is the D-shaped torsion box, used on nearly all his designs (and used by R. S. Mitchell for his Supermarine Spitfire wing), which not only had to carry all loads normally carried by the spar, but also served to give shape to the front portion of the wing. This method was first used in 1921 by the Hannover Akaflieg, or academic flying group, on its wooden Vampyr, but was first used in metal by Messerschmitt. Another typical example will be found later on in the Bf 108 Taifun (Typhoon), where one particular structure had to play three roles: namely, the connection between fuselage and wings, that between fuselage and engine mount, and that between fuselage and landing gear. Further weight was saved by replacing the fuselage formers with the bent edges of the fuselage skin-plates.

Another aspect of BFW at Augsburg, taken in the summer. Seven U 12 Flamingos are in evidence plus, nearest the camera, the BFW 1 Sperber

Discussing a problem at Augsburg: from left to right, Theo Croneiss, Willy Messerschmitt and Otto Strohmeyer. In the background, a BFW-built Flamingo

To save weight, Messerschmitt always took full advantage of the available height or space, for example positioning the spar where the wing profile had its maximum thickness. On his first gliders, he had already used 2-mm wire to manufacture the starting hook, whereas others had used 6-mm thick forged steel. He never tolerated any superfluous material, and when strength calculations did not give him enough information he made a series of load tests which allowed him to use the least material possible. Suppliers of engines and parts would face an irate Messerschmitt every time they dared to supply something heavier than had been expected.

Very early on in his career, Messerschmitt had recognized minimum aerodynamic drag as a determining factor in the advancement of aviation. Even at a time when the biplane formula was being widely used, he remained convinced that to build biplanes was a retrograde step. He was almost fanatical in his attempts to discover different sources of unnecessary drag, and in reducing to the smallest area possible all surfaces exposed to the airstream. For the same reason, he kept the wings of his aircraft as small as possible and thus had to make the fuselage slightly longer than normal, giving him the benefit of smaller elevators and rudders. For a long time, the fixed landing gear was a thorn in his flesh, consisting as it did of a large number of exposed, drag-inducing parts. He did not rest until he had developed his own patented single-leg (cantilever) retractable landing gear. He always studied in great detail all fairings between wings and fuselage, so as to keep interference drag to a minimum. Thus, it is no wonder that Messerschmitt's aircraft usually proved faster than their competitors.

Messerschmitt has said: 'The designer does not only see the aircraft that is flying today, or even the aircraft that is being built or that exists only as a project. No, he looks much further into the future. Long before an aircraft is finished, he knows how it could have been improved. Our work will never cease.' This clearly illustrates Messerschmitt's will to continue improving and developing each aircraft, in contrast to the many designers who drop a design at the first setback rather than improving it systematically even in its smallest details.

It is hardly surprising that Messerschmitt's Projektbüro was always working at top capacity. In fact, his mania for continually improving his aircraft was to lead to violent arguments later on with Göring and Milch, who were to reproach him that he slowed down production with his eternal modifications, even on nearly finished aircraft.

Anything progressive concerned with aviation always gained Messerschmitt's full interest; for example, Fritz von Opel's early experiments with rockets. On 30th September 1929, von Opel made the first rocket-propelled flight in a 'powered-glider', achieving a speed of 85 mph over a distance of $1\frac{1}{4}$ miles before he finally crash-landed. Early in the 1930s, Messerschmitt predicted that aircraft would only become economically feasible when they had become 'unheimlich schnell' or uncannily fast.

At the request of DLH, Messerschmitt developed from the M 18 the M 20, a metal high-wing monoplane capable of carrying 10 passengers. During its first flight, on 26th February 1928, the prototype crashed after a part of the wing fabric tore loose. The pilot tried jumping from an altitude of some 250

The M 20 prototype before its first flight. It could carry an impressive payload of up to 90 per cent of its empty weight

Photo: via Deutsches Museum

A bad omen for the M 20's career: the first flight of the prototype on 26th February 1928 ended in a fatal crash, causing the death of its test pilot, Hans Hackmack

feet but was killed in the attempt. As a result, Luft Hansa's order for two aircraft of this type was immediately cancelled.

Five months later, on 3rd August 1928, the second prototype was test-flown, this time by Theo Croneiss. When all the tests had been concluded successfully, DLH bought its two aircraft and ordered 10 more. But before all of these had been delivered, two of the DLH M 20s crashed. In one incident, the eight occupants, all Reichswehr officers, perished: the accident was heavily dramatized in the newspapers and even discussed in the German Reichstag. DLH's Milch immediately cancelled all the contracts with Messerschmitt and refused to take delivery of the remaining M 20s until the cause of the accidents had been discovered.

This was a considerable financial blow to Messerschmitt, and from this period stemmed the future enmity between the two men. Milch claimed that Messerschmitt incorporated too small a safety factor in his designs, and accused him of showing a lack of feeling for the victims of the accidents. When all possible causes of the accidents had been investigated, it transpired that the M 20 fulfilled all the official strength requirements but that one of these was of insufficient strength to prevent the rudder giving way under heavy loads. This requirement was quickly doubled!

Luft Hansa eventually took delivery of the remaining aircraft, some of which were to serve regularly until 1937. BFW built a total of fourteen M 20s, one of them going to the Brazilian airline company, Empresa de Viação Aerea Rio Grandense, known as VARIG. Two versions were built – the M 20a with a 600-hp BMW engine and the M 20b with a 700-hp BMW.

An M 20 before delivery to Luft Hansa

Photo: Bundesarchiv

An M 20 dwarfing an M 17

An M 20b, D-1928 (W.Nr. 442) being loaded with freight at Düsseldorf airport. This is the windowless freighter version, used by Luft Hansa and called Rheinpfalz (Rhine State)

Photo: via Düsseldorf Town Archives

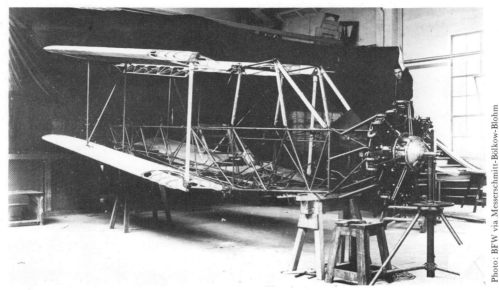

The first prototype of the M 21 under construction. The folding wings are clearly visible

After the financially disastrous M 20 came Messerschmitt's first attempt at building military aircraft. With a view to building up a secret air force, the RVM gave BFW an order to develop a trainer and a bomber. The ex-military pilots responsible for the order insisted that these aircraft be biplanes, although to Messerschmitt this was a retrograde step. The trainer, the M 21, was a development of the BFW 3a Marabu (Stork). (This was almost identical to the U 12 Flamingo, apart from a steel-tube fuselage, bench-type tabs above the

The M 21 just before its first flight. Like the BFW 1 and BFW 3, this type was also unable to supplant the popular Flamingo

BFW's first venture into the field of military aircraft: the unsuccessful M 22, a night-bomber more or less camouflaged as a mail carrier

ailerons, and forward-hinged radius rods to a modified main undercarriage.) Its wings could be folded backwards for storage. Only two prototypes were built – the M 21a with a 96-hp Siemens engine, and the M 21b with a 125-hp Siemens. One prototype only was built of the bomber, the M 22. This twin-engine biplane was built in 1929 but was lost during a test-flight in the summer of 1930, when one of the three-blade propellers flew apart at a height of 6,000 ft. The pilot Eberhardt Mohnicke jumped from the disabled aircraft, but his para-

Another view of the M 22. It crashed during a test flight in the summer of 1930, dragging its pilot, Mohnicke, to his death

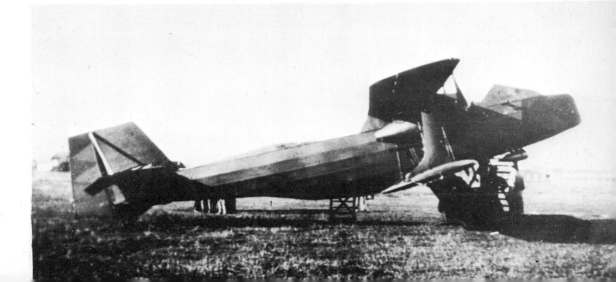

A bevy of BFW aircraft, mostly M 18s, M 20s and M 23s, many belonging to Theo Croneiss's Nordbayerische Verkehrsflug

chute caught on the aircraft and he crashed to his death. The M 22 was officially known as a mail-plane and was one of the first aircraft to be ordered by Germany's clandestine air force. Similar orders were also received by Arado, Albatros and Heinkel.

Some measure of the importance of BFW at this time is given by the fact that of the 450 aircraft registered in Germany in the beginning of 1928, some 37 or 8 per cent were Messerschmitt or BFW types. Flamingos alone accounted for more than 30.

But Messerschmitt's success in the field of military aircraft was still to come.

At the Internationale Luftfahrt Ausstellung, the international aircraft exhibition held in Berlin during October 1928, Messerschmitt showed the M 20a, the M 21b and also the M 23a. The latter was a sporting aircraft designed specifically to compete in the Ostpreussenflug of 1929, organized by the DLV. An all-wood, low-wing two-seater, it had been developed from the M 19 and was to become one of the most popular light aircraft in Germany during the early 1930s, alongside the Klemm monoplanes. It was the first Messerschmitt design to be built in any quantity.

Cutaway drawings of the M 20, the M 22 and the M 23 (from the *Messerschmitt-Typenbuch*)

D-1743 (W.Nr. 451), an M 23a powered by a French Salmson engine. This aircraft was later reregistered as D-EHUH. It was one of the earliest M 23s to be built by BFW

The prototype had a 24-hp Daimler (Ger.) engine, but the series aircraft were equipped with a 34-hp ABC Scorpion II or a 40-hp Salmson (Fr.). The first version, the M 23a, was exhibited at Olympia, London, in 1929, but without great success as no M 23s were ever sold in England. The next version, the M 23b, had a rounded and more streamlined fuselage, and could be equipped with engines of up to 115 hp. One of these aircraft was tried on floats. In 1930, Messerschmitt 'hotted-up' the M 23: the result was the M 23c, which had an enclosed cabin for two passengers, and a metal fuselage front section.

However, it was the M 23b version which was to be built in the largest quantities and which was to meet with success after success. Flown by Croneiss, it won the Ostpreussenflug for which the original M 23 had been designed. Shortly afterwards, flown by Fritz Morzik, it took first place in the Challenge de Tourisme International, the European Rally which the French Aero Club organized for the first time in 1929: no fewer than ten M 23s took part in this event. Still in 1929, Willy Stör took part in the Kunstflug-Meisterschaft, the German National Aerobatics contest held in Essen-Mühlheim, and gained second place behind Gerhard Fieseler flying one of his own designs. The European Rally of 1930 saw eight M 23s taking part; once again Fritz Morzik took first place over 60 competitors, this time flying an M 23c with an enclosed cabin. In September 1930, the pilot Weichelt flew an M 23 upside down for 47 minutes and set up a new record.

In November 1930, Ernst Udet took an M 23b, a Klemm L 25 and a de

An M 23c, D-1884 (W.Nr. 519) powered by the Argus As 8 engine

Two M 23bs taking part in the wing-folding test on Orly airfield, during the 1929 Challenge de Tourisme International. D-1668 (W.Nr. 460) was flown by Theo Croneiss

Photo: Flight International

From May to October 1932, Ernst Udet provided the aerial sequences for the film *S.O.S. Iceberg*, starring Leni Riefenstahl in Greenland. This photograph shows his float-equipped M 23 surrounded by Eskimos, and was taken by Udet from his float-equipped Klemm L 26. He later worked with Riefenstahl on another of her classics, *The White Hell of Pitz Palu*, which featured the Flamingo

Havilland D.H.60 Moth to Africa, in order to make a film. Two years later, again for a film, he took an M 23b and a Klemm L 26, both on floats, and his D.H.60 Moth to Greenland. In 1933, Erwin Aichele and his wife spent their

An unidentified M 23b in front of a hangar at Plauen airfield. Nazi propaganda is very much in evidence: 'Join the Motorized Corps'

Willy Stör flying D-1856 (W.Nr. 514), an M 23b powered by an Argus As 8

honeymoon flying around the Mediterranean in an M 23b, recording a flight of
no fewer than 8,000 miles. Rudolf Hess, Hitler's secretary, was so taken with the
M 23 that he managed to persuade the publishers of the *Völkischer Beobachter*,
the Nazi party's official organ, to buy him one so that he could follow Hitler
on his many propaganda trips. It had the words *Völkischer Beobachter* painted in
large letters on its fuselage.

The M 23b was very light to fly and highly manoeuvrable, although as it had

Upside-down: Willy Stör and his M 23b. Stör later became the German aerobatic champion,
in both 1935 and 1936

Photo: Wolf Hirth

In 1934, a German expedition including Wolf Hirth, Peter Riedel, Heini Dittmar, Hanna Reitsch and Prof. Georgii went to South America to demonstrate gliding. To tow the gliders, an M 23b (W.Nr. 559) registered D-2152 was taken along, equipped with a special towing device. Here it is, taking off with Flugkapitän Wachsmuth at the controls

no brakes or trimmer it was not very easy to land. It was a sporting aircraft in the fullest sense, and as such was very popular in Germany[1]. Altogether, more than seventy M 23s were built – a giant step for Messerschmitt and BFW.

The M 23 was also built under licence in Romania by I.C.A.R. (Întreprinderea de construcţii aeronautice româneşti) of Bucharest, as the I.C.A.R.-M 23b of 1932. In the same year, one of these, flown by Mihail Pantazi and Gheorghe Grozea, bettered the world duration record for floatplanes of less than 500 kg (1,100 lb) in weight by staying in the air for 12 hours 3 minutes.

Some Me 23s were also used at the secret training centre of the embryo German air force at Lipetzk in the USSR.

When Britain's weekly magazine *Flight* published an article on the BFW M 23, on 21st March 1930, it stated: 'Herr Messerschmitt is one of the rising

---

[1] It is noteworthy, however, that its direct competitor, the Klemm L 25 – another low-wing two-seater – was in fact far more successful. Some 600 L 25s were built in Germany, and it was also built under licence in the USA and in England. For this licence construction, the Aeromarine-Klemm Corporation was formed in New York, with works in Keyport, New Jersey, while in Great Britain the British Klemm Aeroplane Co. Ltd. was incorporated at Hanworth Air Park, Feltham, Middlesex.

Photo: Wolf Hirth

In the Argentine in 1934: Peter Riedel, pouring fuel into D-2152's fuel tank, has landed somewhere in the pampas and is being retrieved by Wolf Hirth

Another retrieval . . . Heini Dittmar, the first man to fly faster than 1,000 km/h, is in the rear seat. Quite a day for the gauchos

Photo: Wolf Hirth

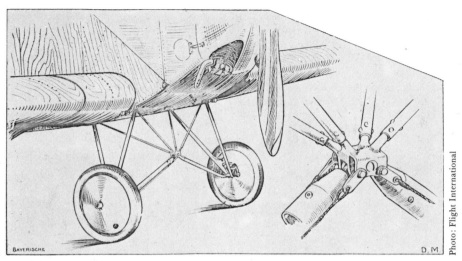

Photo: Flight International

Sketch of the M 23's split undercarriage, with the bent axles hinged to a pyramid from the bottom of the fuselage, from *Flight*, 1929

German designers, and the BFW firm, under his technical direction, has proved itself an energetic and enterprising concern.' Walter Mittelholzer, the well-known Swiss pilot, had this to say about the M 23: 'During the Aircraft Exhibition in Geneva I had the occasion to fly the M 23 at Cointrin and

An M 23b on a fine day in 1929

Dübendorf airfields. Its extraordinarily good handling qualities surprised me, and I can say that when it comes to flying I have never flown a better or more agile aircraft. Equipped with the 80-hp [Armstrong Siddeley] Genet [UK] engine, the machine climbs like a modern fighter and turns steeply without side-slipping. Above all, aerobatic flying is very simple. The machine aerobats with an elegance that one expects only from high-powered fighters. The good gliding performance is surprising and gives the pilot an extraordinary feeling of safety.'

In 1929 Messerschmitt built the M 24. This was an all-metal airliner capable of carrying eight passengers; in fact, a smaller version of the M 20. Two examples of the first version, the M 24a, were built; one had a Junkers L-5 engine and the other a BMW Va. Of the second version, the M 24b, only one was built, equipped with a Pratt & Whitney Hornet engine. For some time, this was tried out on twin floats. Although Messerschmitt had designed this aircraft with a multitude of tasks in view, such as carrying passengers, newspaper transport, aerial photography, as an ambulance, and so on, it did not meet with success, and since the company was experiencing some financial difficulties its construction and development were stopped.

During the winter of 1928–9, Udet had considered replacing his Udet U 12 Flamingo (registered D-822) which he used extensively in flying displays. Indeed, he had used his Flamingo for four years now and it was becoming so well-known all over Germany that some of the novelty was wearing off. He thought of having a special aerobatic biplane built by BFW to his instructions. He discussed these plans with Erich Baier, his personal mechanic, and together they drew up some specifications, Baier making the necessary calculations. Udet then wrote to Messerschmitt about the project, which BFW subsequently designated M 25. After he had used his Flamingo for filming *Die weisse Hölle vom Piz Palü (The White Hell of Piz Palü)*, in Switzerland during February and March 1929, Udet flew his aircraft to Augsburg to be overhauled by BFW. At the same time, he discussed the new aerobatic machine with Messerschmitt and some of the BFW staff. However, nothing came of these plans, as a few months later Udet bought F. O. Soden's de Havilland D.H. 60 Genet Moth (registered G-EBOU, which went on the German register as D-1651 in June 1929).

In the meantime, BFW had been negotiating with companies of various countries with a view to selling the licence rights of the M 18. This aircraft attracted the interest of companies in Switzerland, Estonia, Latvia, Lithuania and the USA. Here, the Eastern Aircraft Corporation (EACO) bought the licence rights, and in addition asked Messerschmitt to design a three-seater touring aircraft which they wanted to build in the USA during the next six years.

The M 26 prototype. It was planned that this type would be built in the USA by the Eastern
Aircraft Corporation. But only this prototype was built, at Augsburg. No production followed

In this way, the M 26, an all-metal shoulder-wing monoplane, was developed
from the M 18. The first prototype was built in Augsburg and was test-flown
in 1930; the 100-hp Siemens gave it a cruising speed of 90 mph. But the big plans
made in the USA all came to nothing when the Eastern Aircraft Corporation
found itself in financial difficulties after the New York Exchange crash on
'Black Friday'.

A staunch advocate of metal construction, Messerschmitt next tried to
improve upon the M 23 by developing the M 27, with a steel-tube fuselage for

The M 27 prototype shortly before its first flight

Photo: Messerschmitt Archiv

The unsuccessful M 28 mailplane D-2059 (W.Nr. 527), equipped with a BMW Hornet engine

its wooden wings. A few were built with the 88-hp Siemens engine (M 27a) and 10 with the 120-hp Argus (M 27b). On this latter version, Messerschmitt tried for the first time the Handley Page slats, an aerodynamic novelty first used in Germany on the Udet U 8.

During 1930, Messerschmitt received another order from DLH – it would prove to be the last one ever. Luft Hansa wanted a fast mail carrier with a large radius of action. The resulting M 28 was designed as a high-wing aircraft but was built as a low-wing monoplane. With its 525-hp BMW it cruised at 160 mph and had a range of 1,500 miles. It was equipped with large fuel tanks; in an emergency, fuel could be dropped very fast, the fuel flowing through the hollow landing-gear axles. Only one of this type was built. It made its first test-flight early in 1931 and remained in service with Luft Hansa until 1935, when it was taken to the Berlin Aviation Museum. Here it was destroyed along with so many other interesting aircraft during an air-raid in the Second World War. Luft Hansa gave an identical order to Focke-Wulf, who developed their FW A 36, equipped with a Pratt & Whitney Hornet of 525 hp.

On 1st January 1930, Kurt Tank joined BFW as director of the Projektbüro.

Photo: BFW

Construction at the Augsburg plant in 1930. The M 26 is in the foreground, on the left

A contemporary of Messerschmitt, Tank left the company the next summer because of its ensuing financial difficulties, and later became world-famous for his Focke-Wulf designs. Unlike Messerschmitt, he was not interested in ultra-light construction. He was more concerned with safety than with the utmost performance of an aircraft.

4
Bankrupt...

The development of the various new types cost a great deal of money which could not be recovered, as the production series were too small. Even when turnover was increased by 40 per cent in 1928, no profit was made and in fact a loss was incurred to the extent of 280,000 RM. However, BFW succeeded in obtaining from the RVM a so-called development subsidy of 200,000 RM, and by reactivating unlisted reserves the balance on 31st December 1928 showed a profit of 1,600 RM.

During 1929, licence contracts were drawn up with the Baltic States (Lithuania, Latvia and Estonia) and, as already noted, with the Eastern Aircraft Corporation of Pawtucket, Rhode Island, USA. The American company obtained licence rights for both the M 18 and the M 26 on the following basis: a single payment of $50,000 was made for the M 18, to be augmented by $300 to $500 for each aircraft built; for the M 26 the agreed sums were $30,000 and $150 to $250. However, because of the financial crash of Wall Street in 1929 and EACO's ensuing financial difficulties, the contract was cancelled after a single payment of $189,000.

Notwithstanding the sale of licence rights, BFW's financial situation deteriorated increasingly during 1929. More subsidies were obtained, and more foreign capital had to be raised. By the following year, 1930, the economic situation in Germany had become catastrophic. Millions of unemployed formed an ideal hotbed for Nazism, while most aircraft manufacturing firms found themselves in a critical situation. Besides BFW, Junkers, Heinkel, Dornier and Arado also had to apply for subsidies. By the end of 1930, BFW had incurred

Photo: Oskar Rumler

Four BFW aircraft at Schleissheim airfield: D-1820, an M 23b in which Strehle and his mechanic Steidle were killed when they crashed into the Taunus mountains on their way to a flying display; D-1881, an M 23 flown by Willy Stör; D-1329, a U 12a Flamingo used by the Luftpolizei (air police); and D-1891, an M 23c flown by Kruger in the 1930 Challenge de Tourisme International, with the competition number 'E 8'

losses to the extent of some 600,000 RM. This the Strohmeyer-Raulino family tried to wipe out by injecting 250,000 RM into the company, while all unlisted reserves and values were reactivated as high as possible. Because of the hopeless situation, BFW's commercial manager, Fritz Hille, resigned and was replaced by Franz Habbel.

Incessantly, the company applied to the RVM and the Bavarian State for additional funds. But for the rest of the German aviation industry, many of whose designers and industrialists had been active during the First World War, BFW was a newcomer and thus an outsider. They used their influence to ensure that no more subsidies were forthcoming for BFW. Some aircraft companies even tried to make use of BFW's difficult position to gain control of the company. The RVM encouraged talks between BFW and Heinkel and Dornier, but no agreement could be reached.

A final blow was dealt to BFW in the spring of 1931, when two M 20s crashed, one at Dresden and the other at Breslau. Immediately, Luft Hansa cancelled its order for 10 of these aircraft and demanded a refund of the down payment. As the production of the M 20 series had already progressed quite far, and a great deal of money had been invested, BFW could not meet the demand.

There was now no way out but to start bankruptcy procedures at the court in Augsburg, on 1st June 1931. The first priority was to attempt to salvage and retain intact the plant's equipment and valuable assets, so as to make a new start possible at a later date. Konrad Merkel was named as the administrator of the estate and together with the commercial manager Rakan Kokothaki, a true Münchener of Cypriotic descent, he tried his utmost to keep the firm going and to make a new start possible.

Even though BFW had gone bankrupt, Messerschmitt Flugzeugbau still existed as a dormant company and now regained some importance as it held the ownership of all Messerschmitt's patents. Every effort possible was now made to reactivate this company, which had absolutely no cash at hand. In order to raise money, Kokothaki even sold his car for 2,000 RM. Some time later, the licence rights for the M 23c were sold in Romania for 6,000 RM, so that in the autumn of 1931 a capital of 8,000 RM was available.

In the meantime, Konrad Merkel had succeeded in making Luft Hansa honour its order for the M 20 and M 28 aircraft, as it had been proved that the M 20 crashes could not be attributed to any fault on the part of BFW or Messer-schmitt. However, the fact that Erhard Milch, the director of Luft Hansa and later to become Field Marshal and Secretary of State for the Air Ministry, had withdrawn the order in the first place, and the ensuing quarrel, led to a deep-seated and long-lasting hostility between Milch and Messerschmitt. This state of affairs was not helped at all by the fact that Messerschmitt was a friend of

Photo: via Lufthansa

An M 20b standing in front of the BFW works at Augsburg, before being delivered to Luft Hansa

Theo Croneiss, whose Nordbayerische Verkehrsflug was the only serious rival to Luft Hansa.

The very existence of BFW was again threatened in 1932, when a notable creditor of the company, the city of Augsburg, announced its intentions of obtaining the BFW factory to use it as a depot for its streetcars. It is said that Rudolf Hess, a former First World War fighter pilot with whom Messerschmitt had become acquainted when he bought an M 23b, and who already enjoyed a very high status within the Nazi party, used his influence to thwart this attempt to oust Messerschmitt from his own factory. Another dangerous moment came when Ernst Heinkel proposed that the city of Augsburg should sell the plant and all BFW's equipment to him, promising in return that he would hire a fixed number of workmen and other employees.

However, an agreement was eventually reached between all the creditors at a preliminary meeting in December 1932. This agreement was officially testified on 27th April 1933 at an Augsburg court. Thus, on 1st May 1933, BFW AG was able to reopen and start anew, even though it was left with only 82 employees. Unlike other German manufacturing firms which managed to survive, BFW was forced to start again practically from scratch. The bankruptcy caused a loss of some 900,000 RM to the Michel-Raulino family.

During this trying period, the well-known yearbook *Jane's All the World's Aircraft* wrote: 'The BFW Company has found itself in difficulties. For the time being, therefore, its affairs are being handled by the Messerschmitt Flugzeugbau GmbH of the same address.'

In the midst of all this financial reorganization, Messerschmitt received an order to develop a sports aircraft for the third European Rally of 1932. This Challenge de Tourisme was organized to stimulate the development of practical touring aircraft. For this, Messerschmitt designed and built the racy-looking M 29, a low-wing monoplane with wooden wings and a steel-tube fuselage, powered by a 150-hp Argus and seating two in tandem in an enclosed cockpit.

The aircraft which were to take part in the rally were finished only a few weeks before the event took place, and the competing pilots only had one week in which to become acquainted with a new type that was far from easy to fly. Amongst other things, it was one of the first modern types to be equipped with an all-flying tail. While training on 8th August 1932, one of the pilots, Kreuzkamp, crashed to his death from an altitude of 2,000 feet. The following day, another M 29 failed in the air. The pilot Poss was able to parachute to safety, but the mechanic died in the crash. As a result of these two accidents, the M 29 was not allowed to participate in the Challenge. It was discovered later on that the failures were due to vibrations originating in the horizontal stabilizer.

Altogether, five M 29s were built, supplemented by one M 29b powered by a 150-hp Siemens engine. These aircraft were of an advanced concept, being equipped with flaps, Handley Page slats and single (cantilever) legs for the main landing gear; all of which were still novelties at this time. Notwithstanding a maximum speed of 262 km/h (163 mph), the landing speed was as low as 55 km/h (34 mph). Although the M 29 was ordered at a fixed price, an unusual procedure at that time, Messerschmitt GmbH was still able to obtain a comfortable profit on this type.

Next came a number of designs which, for the most part, were to remain projects.

The M 30 was a project based on the M 26, and was to be built in magnesium in the USA. It was never built.

The M 31 progressed a little further, as one prototype was built. With this project, Messerschmitt aimed to introduce a very cheap sportsplane, as he

Photo: Messerschmitt Archiv

An M 29b; this type was developed for the 1932 Challenge de Tourisme International but after two wing failures on two consecutive days it was banned from participating

The only M 31 to be built. Good performance, good looks, but no production

A mock-up of BFW's 'week-end amphibium', the M 32, exhibited at the DELA in Berlin, September 1932. This far-out project – which was not designed by Messerschmitt – was never constructed

thought this would stand a good chance in a time of great misery and economic depression. It was an improved but greatly simplified version of the M 23, powered by a 60-hp BMW engine and kept as plain as possible in order to keep the price down. The only springing or shock absorption in the landing gear was provided by the tyres. However, BMW decided not to produce their 60-hp engine and this meant the end of the M 31.

The M 32 was not designed by Messerschmitt himself, and was a fantastic and futuristic project, built only as a mock-up. It was to have been a 'week-end' amphibian, equipped with a retractable caterpillar-track landing gear. Power was to be supplied by two Diesel engines, while a rocket was to be fitted to assist take-off.

The M 33 was another novel project, but this time an extremely cheap single-seater powered by a 15-hp DKW car engine. BFW planned to sell it as a kit to home-builders. It was an amusing design, the pilot being seated in a pod below the wing. Only a mock-up was built, and this was exhibited at the 1932 Deutsche Luftsport-Ausstellung (DELA), a national sports-flying aircraft exhibition held in Berlin, together with the M 31, a mock-up of the M 32, and a model of the M 34.

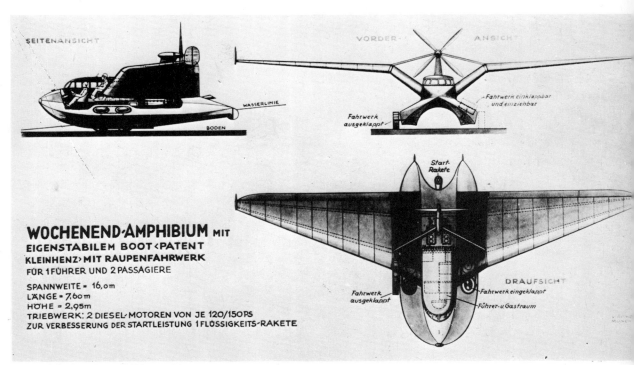

Week-end amphibium with auto-stable hull (Kleinhenz patent) and tracked undercarriage, for one pilot and two passengers. Drawings show ground-level and water-line, and the undercarriage lowered (left) and retracted and enclosed (right). Span: 52 ft; length: 25 ft; height: 9 ft; two Diesel engines of 120-150 hp each; one liquid rocket to improve take-off

The M 33, another BFW brainchild that was built only as a mock-up. It was an ultra-light sports aircraft which was to be sold in kit-form. Here it is as exhibited at the DELA in Berlin 1932

Everyone his own aircraft builder! The M 33 in a building kit. Span: 30 ft; length: 18 ft; height: 6 ft; one 15-hp two-stroke DKW engine 'Type P'

The M 34 project was for a very long-range aircraft, powered by two Diesel engines buried in the fuselage, which together were to drive one propeller mounted on an outrigger on top of the fuselage. The M 34 would have had a cruising speed of 350 km/h (217 mph) and a range of 20,000 km, roughly half the world's circumference or 12,500 miles. Hence its name: 'Antipode-Aircraft'.

5
A Nation of Aviators[1]

On the night of 30th January 1933, thousands upon thousands of SS and SA men, carrying flaming torches, paraded through the streets of Berlin before the newly elected Chancellor, Adolf Hitler. Beside him stood Hermann Göring – a First World War fighter 'ace' who was now one of the most influential men in the Nazi party, and was destined to become Minister for the German Ministry of Aviation, the Reichsluftfahrtministerium (RLM) which came into being on 27th April 1933.

Freedom came to an end in Germany, but aviation was to benefit from an unsurpassed and unique development.

Almost immediately every aircraft manufacturing company received huge contracts and financial help for their development . . . except BFW. They received an order to build 12 Heinkel He 45Cs under licence, nothing else. The man responsible for giving the orders at the RLM was Erhard Milch, and he, as we have seen, carried no torch for Messerschmitt. He paid no attention to Messerschmitt's own designs, and simply ordered him to manufacture under licence an aircraft designed by one of his fiercest rivals.

BFW was powerless to do anything about this most unpleasant situation, and thus began to make preparations for the construction of the He 45Cs. To this end, some BFW representatives, including Kokothaki, went to the Heinkel factory at Warnemünde to obtain the necessary information. To their great

---

[1] '. . . Germany shall become a nation of aviators' – Göring speaking on 24th June 1934.

surprise, they were not even allowed inside the Heinkel workshops, where they had hoped to carry out a full inspection of the aircraft they were to construct. Only after the RLM had exerted considerable pressure were they shown the He 45C – not in the workshops, but in an open field.

Meanwhile, in the spring of 1933, Messerschmitt's design bureau had little work to do, and so in June Kokothaki went to Bucharest, Romania, to try to obtain an order for designing a transport aircraft. After some negotiations, the Romanian factory I.C.A.R. asked BFW to design a high-wing aircraft with capacity for six passengers and two crew members, to be powered by a 450-hp Gnôme-et-Rhône engine. This commission resulted in the M 36, which was, however, powered by a 380-hp Armstrong Siddeley Serval Mark I. With a cruising speed of 220 km/h (137 mph), it was the first transport aircraft to be built in Romania, where it carried the designation I.C.A.R.-Comercial. The M 36 specification was timely and prevented BFW from losing its last designers and kept alive a small development department.

Also in June, Croneiss and Seiler tried to influence Milch and get him to help BFW by placing substantial orders with the company. Milch countered by saying that although he considered Messerschmitt to be one of the most capable aircraft designers in the world, he still reproached him for 'not daring to show his face' after the Luft Hansa M 20 crashes. As a condition against any further orders, he demanded from BFW a cautionary sum of no less than 2,000,000 RM, to be paid within 24 hours of any crash involving any new aircraft designed by Messerschmitt. To Milch's utmost surprise, Seiler calmly accepted his terms. The immediate result of this agreement was an order to build 30 Dornier Do 11 bombers under licence. The construction of these bombers, together with the Heinkel aircraft, allowed BFW to expand considerably at Augsburg, and soon more than five hundred men were employed by the company. However, despite this the relationship between Milch and Messerschmitt did not improve, especially when in October 1933 Milch ran into trouble over his supposed

YR-ACS, the M 36 built in Romania. It served from 1936 to 1938 on internal Romanian airlines. I.C.A.R. planned a tri-motor version but nothing came of it

Jewish descent, trouble which he believed to have originated from Theo Croneiss, who in the meantime had risen to a high position with the SA.

Unlike Croneiss, Messerschmitt had neither time for nor interest in politics. On the design side, in 1932, Messerschmitt engaged Ing. Robert Lusser, who

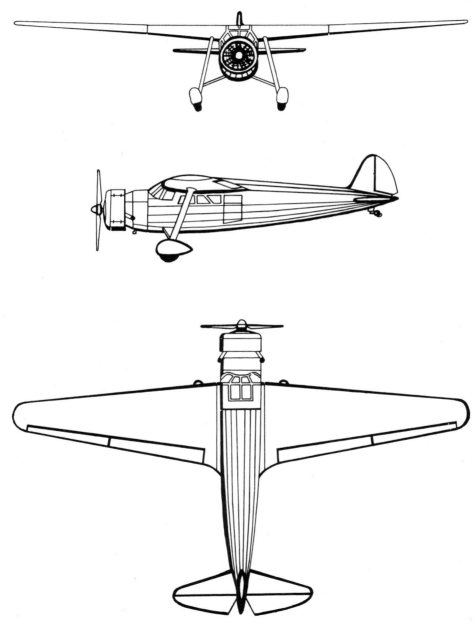

Three-view drawing of the M 36

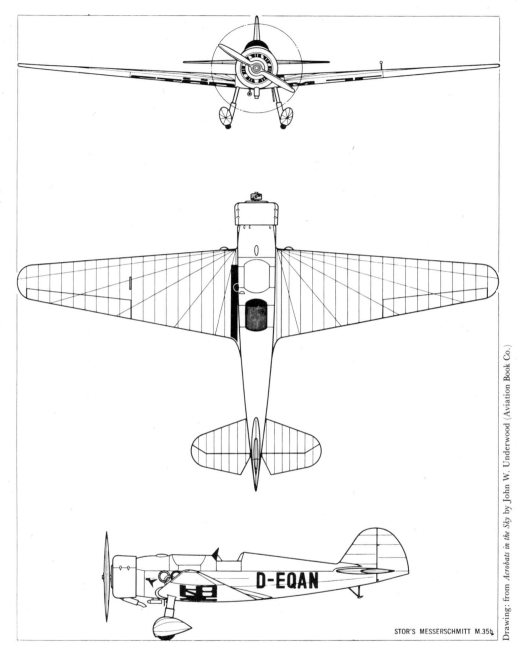

STOR'S MESSERSCHMITT M.35b

Drawing: from *Acrobats in the Sky* by John W. Underwood (Aviation Book Co.)

Three-view drawing of Willy Stör's M 35b

had previously worked with Hans Klemm. Lusser stayed only a short while with BFW, departing to join the service of Heinkel. At the end of 1933, Messerschmitt appointed a new chief-engineer, Walter Rethel, who had already

D-3420 (W.Nr. 626): an M 35 powered by a Siemens-Halske Sh 14a and used by the DVS

gained a great deal of experience designing fast aircraft for Arado.

Making full use of the experience he had gained with the M 29 and the M 31, Messerschmitt now designed a low-wing monoplane especially suited to aerobatics. Designated the M 35, 'for instruction, touring or sport', this was a beautiful two-seater with a steel-tube fuselage and wooden wings. A true thoroughbred, it enchanted every pilot who had the opportunity to handle it. All told, some fifteen M 35s were built, only two of which were to the original two-seat instructional specification, the majority being aerobatic single-seaters. Messerschmitt indulged his design preference for the simple cantilever main undercarriage legs, in this case with wide track and streamlined wheel spats or covers incorporating a patented pneumatic shock-absorber. Normally, the M 35 was powered by a 150-hp Siemens, but one example was equipped with a 225-hp Argus.

In February 1935, Rudolf Hess, now the second man in the Nazi party, piloted an M 35 in the Zugspitzflug, a race from Munich to Germany's highest mountain, the Zugspitze, and back. This was an annual event and had been won by Hess the previous year. He flew under the pseudonym of 'Müller', his navigator being von Wurmb. In both 1935 and 1936 Willy Stör became the aerobatic champion of Germany, flying an M 35. After the championship, he declared: 'I owe my victory to the M 35 and its Bramo Sh 14 A engine.[1]' During 1935, Stör demonstrated the M 35 in several countries, including

---

[1] The Sh aircraft engines were manufactured by Siemens & Halske AG, Flugmotorenwerk of Spandau near Berlin. In 1936 this company became the Brandenburgische Motorenwerke; some Sh engines were kept in production and prefixed Bramo – Bra + Mo – rather than Sh.

Willy Stör demonstrating his 'sun-burst'-pattern aerobatic M 35

Hungary, Italy, Bulgaria, Yugoslavia and Romania. Although the aircraft attracted a great deal of interest, no export orders were forthcoming. In 1936, Vera von Bissing became the European aerobatics champion flying an M 35; one of the spectators of this event was Charles Lindbergh.

In the meantime, Messerschmitt's acceptance of the M 36 design-order from I.C.A.R. had incurred the wrath of the RLM. The most outspoken critic was Major Wimmer of the Technisches Amt, who argued that at a time when German aviation, civil as well as military, was expanding on such an enormous scale, it ill-behoved a German company to design aircraft for a foreign company, as all existing capacity for both design and production was needed in Germany itself. BFW's reply was not long in coming: it declared that it had been forced to seek orders from abroad because of Milch's hostile attitude, as evidenced by the fact that no substantial orders had been given to the company at home. If BFW were to survive, it was forced to seek orders from abroad. This retort did not miss its target, and, as a direct result, the RLM gave BFW an order to develop a touring aircraft, to be designed specifically for the RLM's participation in the 4th Challenge de Tourisme International of 1934. BFW was also allowed to enter a design competition for a new fighter aircraft; no-one thought the company stood a chance, however, as the other competitors included Heinkel, Focke-Wulf and Arado.

These two decisions were to have far-reaching effects, which no-one could as yet foresee, not the least Erhard Milch. Even in 1933, when acting as Secretary of State, Milch had demanded that the management of BFW be taken over by someone other than Messerschmitt or Kokothaki, neither of these men finding any favour with him whatsoever. Thus, BFW was forced to name Herr Schwartzkopff as the new manager of the company.

In December 1932, BFW had started negotiating with Handley Page over the right to use the Handley Page 'slot'. The outcome was that BFW was allowed to use the slotted wing patented by Handley Page, who in his turn was allowed to use Messerschmitt's patents for single-spar wing construction. As already related, Messerschmitt first used the system on the M 27b.

1933 had been a gloomy year, and in fact BFW showed a loss of some 40,000 RM for the year. However, the prospects for 1934 seemed better, especially when the Technisches Amt at the RLM was taken over by Major Loeb. He was totally unprejudiced against BFW and Messerschmitt, even though Milch's enmity continued, and collaboration between him and Messerschmitt proved to be excellent.

Messerschmitt's design for the RLM's official participation in the 4th Challenge de Tourisme International was the four-seater M 37. In direct competition were the Klemm Kl 36 and the Fieseler Fi 97, both of which were designed against identical specifications from the RLM. The M 37 received the new designation of Bf 108 when the RLM decided that German aircraft manufacturers should no longer be allowed to give random designations to their products. Every manufacturer was allotted its own prefix (thus, Bf for BFW), to be followed by a number which could be used only once, contrary to the former, totally free, system.

When setting out to design the M 37/Bf 108 Messerschmitt used all the latest techniques. The finished aircraft, an all-metal low-wing monoplane with retractable landing gear, was of a very advanced concept indeed. The wings were equipped with flaps, and could be folded against the fuselage. Following his agreement with Handley Page, Messerschmitt again used the slotted-wing device which he had first used on the M 27b. The first six Bf 108s, those that were built for the Challenge, had no ailerons but were instead equipped with spoilers on top of each wing. This system enabled the flaps to be applied over the

Photo: Archiv Schliephake

D-ILIT, one of the first Bf 108s. Note the small ailerons extending aft of the trailing-edge

full length of the trailing edge. All further machines, however, were equipped with classic ailerons. The fuselage was of pure monocoque construction without any stringers.

When a few Bf 108s had been built it transpired that the underside of the fuselage was too weak, and could cause failures when highly stressed. All existing machines had to be modified, and in the meantime all aerobatics were forbidden. However, when Rudolf Hess piloted a Bf 108 for the first time at Berlin's Staaken airfield, he was not told of this decision and calmly tried out one aerobatic figure after another, before some appalled onlookers who expected the machine to crack up at any minute. What Hess said after he landed and was told all has not been recorded.

While training for the Challenge, the pilot Freiherr von Düngern crashed in one of the Bf 108s. The accident was probably caused by the spoilers which, if used when flying slowly, could make one wing stall. Theo Osterkamp, who was responsible for the RLM's participation in the Challenge, wanted to place a ban on all the Bf 108s because of this crash, whereupon BFW tried to have Osterkamp replaced by someone else. A solution was finally found by working day and night and replacing the spoilers with ailerons.

The Challenge was held from 29th August to 14th September 1934, and the participating countries, apart from Germany, were Italy, Czechoslovakia, and Poland, the organizing country. The German entrants were comprised of four Bf 108s, five Fi 97s, and four Kl 36s. Although the Bf 108 was the fastest aircraft taking part, the two first places were taken by Polish pilots flying RWD 9s. The

Photo: Messerschmitt-Bölkow-Blohm

The wing-folding mechanism of the Bf 108

best placed Bf 108 – D-IMUT flown by Theo Osterkamp – came fifth. One of the trials was the derigging, or taking apart, of the machines by two people, and in this the RWD 9s gained many points against the Bf 108s.

Later on, Bf 108s were to achieve many victories and make many remarkable flights. Fräulein Elly Beinhorn, the well-known German aviatrix, flew a Bf 108 from Gleiwitz to Istanbul and back to Berlin in one day, and in 1937 flew one from Berlin to Cape town. Otto Brindlinger, a BFW pilot, flew a Bf 108 from Berlin to Stockholm daily throughout the Olympics of 1936, to assist with the news coverage of the events. In the International Flight of the Oases in 1937 a Bf 108 gained second place, and first places were won by these aircraft

D-IGAK, another of the earliest Bf 108s, equipped with a 225-hp Argus As 17a. It was flown by Francke in the 1934 Challenge de Tourisme International; carrying competition number '15' it is seen here at Evere, the airfield at Brussels, having flown in from Warsaw. Here again, note the ailerons extending aft of the trailing-edge

Caught in the act! One day Otto Brindlinger was flying a Bf 108 above Kitzingen, when along came a Focke-Wulf FW 56 D-IKMC. The camera clicked, but when Ernst Udet saw the photograph he retorted that such 'close formation' had almost lost Brindlinger his flying licence

Photo: via W. Radinger

Elly Beinhorn poses for the Press in front of her Bf 108, after her remarkable flight from Berlin to Istanbul

in the Queen Astrid Rally in Belgium, the Hoggar Rally, the Rally to Dinard, and the Isle of Man Race. In 1939, a Bf 108 set a height record of 9,075 m (29,775 ft). Messerschmitt himself used a Bf 108 for his personal travel needs, registered D-IMTT.

The Luftwaffe ordered some Bf 108s for use as liaison aircraft, and also as trainers for pilots who were later to fly the Bf 109 fighter, about which more will follow. The Bf 108 made its operational debut during the Spanish Civil War, when it was used as a courier aircraft by the Legion Condor, the German volunteer corps.

More than one version of the Bf 108 existed, the first version with the original spoilers and small provisional ailerons being called simply the Bf 108. The type that went into production was the Bf 108 B, powered by a 240-hp Argus. Practically all 108s to be built were of this type, as only one Bf 108 C, an experimental aircraft fitted with a 400-hp Hirth 12-cylinder engine, was ever built.

BFW tried to sell its Bf 108, which it called commercially the Taifun (Typhoon), abroad and for this purpose organized demonstration flights, some of which were real expeditions. On 25th May 1936, a Bf 108 (registered D-IONO),

An unusual air-freighting proposition: a Bf 108, D-IONO, underneath the Zeppelin Lz 129 which transported it to South America.

was even shipped to South America, on board the Zeppelin Lz 129, the ill-fated *Hindenburg*. The following year, in December, another Bf 108 (D-IBFW) was shipped by boat to Rio de Janeiro, Brazil, for a 44,000-km (27,340 miles)-long sales and demonstration tour across South, Central and North America. It was flown by Otto Brindlinger, an ex-First World War pilot, nicknamed 'Rintintin', who was Messerschmitt's foreign sales representative, while the entire undertaking was organized by another member of the Messerschmitt staff, Horst von Salomon. The third and last crew-member was a female journalist and photographer who later wrote a book about the eventful trip, entitled *Eine Frau fliegt mit . . . (A Woman Flies Along . . .)*. At the airfield of Porto Alegre, in Brazil, they came across a veteran Messerschmitt product – an M 20 which, after having served in Luft Hansa (as D-UKIP) had been sold to the Brazilian airline VARIG (registered PP-VAK) and named *Acegua*. Its pilot commented: 'The M 20 is indestructible. It's a wonderfully faithful and reliable animal. Day by day, I use it to fly passengers across the country.' Later on, the team crossed the Andes Mountains, and after several months of flying, demonstrations – and repairs – they reached New York on 5th July 1938. On that day, Brindlinger flew D-IBFW from Brownsville near the Mexican border to Floyd Bennett Field, New York, covering nearly 4,000 km (2,485 miles) – using five refuelling stops – in one single day.

Many Bf 108s were exported; for example: 12 to Switzerland, 9 to Romania, 2 to the Soviet Union, 6 to Bulgaria, 12 to Yugoslavia and a batch to Hungary where they were used by the Hungarian Air Force. Japan used Bf 108s on the Manchurian Air Lines, while the sole example to be exported to England was impressed in September 1939, together with two Bf 108s that had been used by the German Embassy in London; the three machines were used by the RAF as communications aircraft. Amazingly enough, in October 1938, a Bf 108 B-1, D-IQBR, was even bought by the Ernst Heinkel Flugzeugwerke at Rostock.

Otto Brindlinger flying Bf 108 D-IBFW over New York, in July 1938, at the end of the 44,000-km demonstration tour which started at Rio de Janeiro, Brazil. Note the convenient sales impact of the German civil registration – 'BFW'

Many Bf 108s were exported. This one went to Chile

The 108 was a very progressive aircraft when it was first designed, and in fact some surviving examples were still being flown in the early 1970s, nearly forty years after its conception. Even more remarkable is the fact that on 29th November 1973 a company was incorporated, with Professor Messerschmitt as one of its founders, to take up production of the 108 once more, in a slightly improved form.

Every pilot who ever had the chance to fly a Bf 108 had to concede that it was a true thoroughbred, with pleasant handling characteristics, good pilot

Photo: Messerschmitt-Bölkow-Blohm

The comfortable interior of the Bf 108, which does not look out of style in the 1970s

A Bf 108 B after export to Switzerland, where it was used by the Swiss Air Force

visibility, comfort and a nice appearance. As it had been built specifically for the 1934 Challenge, where points were awarded for items such as visibility, safety, comfort, and so on, the 108 represented a break-through in lightplane design. The older sports aircraft were now superseded by touring aircraft. Messerschmitt gained a great deal of valuable experience with the 108, which

The Bf 108's attractively designed cockpit

Messerschmitt's own Bf 108, looking surprisingly modern for a touring aircraft conceived in 1933

he was to use to good avail when designing his next aircraft, the Bf 109 fighter.

To build a touring aircraft in 1934 which could obtain a cruising speed of 265 km/h (165 mph) from a 240-hp engine was an accomplishment which even today does not look at all bad. And in fact, the Bf 108's success proved a considerable moral support to Willy Messerschmitt, who in the course of 1934 had seriously considered leaving the aircraft industry to take up the post of Professor of Aeronautical Construction at the Danzig technical college.

6
1934-1936

After the RLM had, albeit reluctantly, given Messerschmitt permission to take part in the fighter design competition, together with Heinkel, Focke-Wulf and Arado, he started work on this new project – the Bf 109. In Berlin he had been told in no uncertain terms that even if his project did turn out to be the best – which was considered extremely unlikely – he should not count on an order to begin series production of the new fighter. Even so, Messerschmitt decided to risk all and to build a fighter of an advanced concept, making use of the most modern techniques. Characteristics of the Bf 109 were thus to be: all-metal construction, cantilever wings with flaps and automatic slots, monocoque fuselage, retractable single-legged landing gear, totally enclosed cabin, and the smallest possible fuselage section, just big enough to take the most powerful engine available in Germany at that time, the Junkers Jumo 210A. A design team was formed under the direct leadership of Messerschmitt himself, and Dipl. Ing. Rethel.

In the meantime, Air Minister Göring's massive procurement programme for the Luftwaffe was resulting in correspondingly large orders, given to aircraft manufacturing firms all over Germany. BFW expected to receive its share of these, and in order to increase its production capacity bought the engineering firm of Eppel und Buxbaum – not without causing some excitement amongst the owners of the company, in particular Willy Messerschmitt who was not at all convinced that this investment was justified. A total sum of 450,000 RM had to be paid in annual instalments of 50,000 RM over a period of nine years. Initially, doubts were raised as to whether the new capacity would ever be used for building aircraft, but these were soon dispelled; during 1934 the new factory was already being used to full capacity for aircraft construction, and in fact a new manufacturing hall had to be constructed as well. Yet it was during this period that Messerschmitt considered taking up the post of Professor at Danzig (he had lectured on the subject of aircraft construction since 1930, at the technical college at Munich). He inquired of the RLM whether they considered his person to be of some importance to the aircraft procurement programme; they replied that he was not needed at all, and that he would in fact do well to accept the professorship offered. However, some good friends kept Messerschmitt from taking this step.

Whereas BFW's total turnover for 1933 had been 166,000 RM, this figure was increased to 2,616,000 RM in 1934, even though the major part of the company's activity for this year was the licence construction of aircraft designed by other companies. Six Bf 108s were the only self-designed aircraft to be built during 1934. All development capacity was taken up by the design of the Bf 109, and yet at the end of 1934 the design of another new type, the Bf 110, was begun.

The Bf 110 was a twin-engined Kampfzerstörer, a fighter meant to clear the way for attacking bombers. Orders to develop such an aircraft were also given to AGO, Dornier, Henschel, Heinkel, Focke-Wulf, and Gotha. The very concept of the Kampfzerstörer had many opponents, Messerschmitt himself being convinced that the RLM's requirements would not lead to a good design. When working on the 110, together with Dipl. Ing. Rethel, he ignored some of the RLM's recommendations, concentrating all his attention upon the question of obtaining a good performance. Thus he designed a two-seater, rather than a three-seater, and planned for much lighter armament than the RLM had prescribed.

On 1st March 1935, the Luftwaffe threw away its mask, after having existed in secret for some time. The so-called Enttarnung, or 'de-camouflaging', meant that the existence of a German Air Force was no longer disguised: ordering large quantities of new aircraft, building new factories, all this could now be carried out openly.

In the spring of this year, the RLM's Technisches Amt or Technical Office, the department responsible for drawing up specifications for new aircraft, announced a design competition for a liaison aircraft, to be powered by a 240-hp Argus As 10 C engine. Besides BFW, Fieseler and Siebel also submitted designs for this competition, which was ultimately won by the well-known Fieseler Storch (Stork). The BFW project received the BFW project number P 1051 and was designated Bf 163 by the RLM. It came under the direction of Dipl. Ing. Robert Lusser, and closely resembled the Storch. Construction of a prototype was started during the summer. 1935 also saw the start of the development of two types derived from the Bf 110, which had not yet flown itself.

Photo: VFW-Fokker

The carefully made model of the Bf 163, the unsuccessful competitor to the Fieseler Fi 156 Storch. The similarity with the Storch is evident

These were the Bf 161, a reconnaissance version, and the Bf 162, a fast bomber.

However, for Messerschmitt the most important event of the year was the first flight of the Bf 109 prototype, registered D-IABI, early in September. As the Junkers engine was not yet ready, a Rolls-Royce Kestrel driving a two-bladed propeller was installed provisionally. When the BFW test-pilot, 'Bubi' Knötsch took off in the 109 for the first time, from Augsburg airfield, many taxiing tests had already been made, during which a provisional strut had been installed between the two under-carriage legs. After some preliminary testing at Augsburg, Knötsche flew the prototype to the Luftwaffe's testing airfield at Rechlin, where one of the landing-gear legs broke during the landing. The test-pilots at Rechlin had been somewhat wary of the announced Bf 109, because of

Photo: via G. Van Acker

A Bf 109 B-1 with the engine cowling removed

the many novel features incorporated in its design, and their scepticism was of course increased by this unfortunate accident. The following month, the first Jumo 210A was at last delivered and promptly installed in the second prototype. In general, the 109's chances of survival were thought to be very small, the favourite being the Heinkel He 112. Heinkel had already built many good aircraft in large series, whereas Messerschmitt had not yet built a single successful warplane.

The German aircraft industry was being given more and more orders, and during 1935 BFW was able to note down the following:

    32 Bf 108 B
    10 Bf 109
    35 Heinkel He 50
    70 Heinkel He 45 D
    90 Arado Ar 66
    115 Gotha Go 145

Production capacity had to be increased again, and for this purpose a new construction hall was erected – Hangar 4, 2 km ($1\frac{1}{2}$ miles) away from the airfield. Heavy building programmes meant that nearly every German aircraft manufacturing company was desperately short of capital. The banks were hesitant about giving more and more credit and so, to alleviate the situation, the RLM started giving investment credits, which were, however, redeemable at any time. In this way, BFW had borrowed a total of 3.6 million RM from the RLM by the end of 1935. The large sums of credit involved led the RLM to demand in 1936 that BFW increase its capital to 400,000 RM. The RLM wanted the 3.6 million RM credit to become share capital, whereby the German Reich would become the owner of the shares and BFW would lose its independence. After long and difficult discussions, a solution satisfactory to both parties was at last found. BFW increased its capital by 3.6 million marks to 4 million marks on 31st March. A large portion of the shares, in fact 2.1 million RM, were administered by a trustee designated by both the RLM and BFW, namely F. W. Seiler, who had been the president of the shareholders' committee. He also administered the shares of the Raulino family and those owned by the C. Z. Thomsen banking house. With this arrangement, the German Reich could never go over the heads of the private shareholders. It was also agreed that the Reich would sell its shares within the next ten years, at a fixed price, to the private shareholders.

On 12th May, BFW's test-pilot Rudolf Opitz made the first flight with the Bf 110 prototype, taking off from Augsburg airfield. This new type's two powerful engines caused a great deal of trouble during this first test-flight, and in fact

Prof. Willy Messerschmitt in a Bf 108 piloted by Dipl. Ing. Lucht, the Luftwaffe's chief engineer

it was to be another five months before a second Bf 110 prototype could be used in the test programme.

In June 1936 Udet joined the RLM. Since he and Messerschmitt were on friendly terms, the relationship between Messerschmitt and the RLM improved steadily as Udet's influence grew. But in the meantime, the RLM had placed new requirements before Messerschmitt, demanding that BFW increase its capacity to an even greater extent. The City of Augsburg did not approve of such an increase within its territorial limits, and so BFW was forced to buy some real estate at Regensburg, where a completely new factory was erected. Messerschmitt did not want to run the risk of his company falling into the hands of the Reich by taking up considerable credit once more, and so for the new factory a new company was founded on 24th July 1936: the Messerschmitt GmbH. At Augsburg, the experimental workshops, drawing bureaux and administration department were extended, while work on the Regensburg factory continued at a hectic pace. Only seven Bf 108s had been built at Augsburg in 1935, but series production was now organized at Regensburg.

All these extensions, construction and development meant that Messerschmitt had no more time to devote to the Bf 163. Through the RLM, he asked Dr Rohrbach to take care of the project in Berlin. Rohrbach came to Augsburg to inspect the mock-up of the Bf 163 and was anything but enthusiastic, but he was obliged to take on the assignment. Just the one mock-up had been built, and now one delay followed another, at a time when three prototypes of the Fieseler Storch, the Bf 163's direct competitor, were already being test-flown.

Photo: via G. Van Acker

A Bf 109 B-1 equipped with a Jumo 210 D engine and a Schwarz wooden propeller

On 1st August the Olympic Games were officially opened at Berlin, carefully organized to impress all foreign visitors with the might and order of Nazi Germany. The spectators caught a glimpse of the Bf 109 when Ing. Francke flew the second prototype (D-IUDE), over the Olympic stadium, while below the first European television camera filmed the proceedings.

The RLM had in the meantime been showing more and more interest in the Bf 109, so that when the time came for the final official demonstration in the autumn of 1936 at the E-Stelle Travemünde test-centre, no-one could say for certain whether the Bf 109 or the Heinkel He 112 would be chosen. The demonstration of the 109 was given by Dr Ing. Hermann Wurster, who had joined Messerschmitt as a test-pilot in January 1936. The two fighters were first compared for their aerobatic qualities. Here the 109 with its sturdy trapezoidal wing was far more effective than the He 112 with its weaker elliptical wing. Wurster had no qualms about executing twenty-three left-hand consecutive spins, immediately followed by twenty-one consecutive right-hand ones, thereby losing some 5,000 m (16,400 ft) in altitude. As if this was not enough, he then performed a near-vertical dive from 7,000 m (23,000 ft). The Heinkel pilot did not trust his untried 112 sufficiently to emulate Wurster's demonstration. This, and the fact that the 109 was simpler to build than the 112, made the RLM decide: the Bf 109 was to be the Luftwaffe's standard fighter. It alone was to be ordered in quantity. It was a momentous decision.

The decision had been taken in the main by Ernst Udet, now Inspector of the Fighter Pilots, and his friend Ritter von Greim, their General. It was fiercely criticized on several points: the Heinkel fighter was, after all, the faster of the two and also had a better rate of climb; furthermore, some of the 109's weaker points, especially its narrow landing gear, had by now become apparent. However, the RLM stood by the 109, and further decided that in future Messerschmitt was to concentrate on designing and building fighter aircraft, while Heinkel took care of the bombers. This final decision was of course an enormous triumph for Messerschmitt, and production lines for the aircraft were immediately installed at Augsburg. It was to be two years before the RLM expressed any interest in any other fighter; only then would the Focke-Wulf 190 enter the scene.

In order to finance the tremendous growth of the aviation industry, a special bank was set up, the Bank für Luftfahrt, for which capital was made available by both the Finanzministerium, the Ministry of Finance, and the RLM. However, only 35 per cent of the amount available for 1936 was taken up; the various companies involved simply could not be developed quickly enough, and were also loath to take more and more credit from the State, fearing that its influence would lead to problems and a possible loss of independence. Again, many companies were not convinced that the investments would prove profitable when the expansion had been completed. During 1936, BFW had for the most part built aircraft under licence, with only a few of its own designs, the 108 and the 109, coming off the production lines. But now, in this respect, the future looked very rosy.

In June 1936 the man with whom Messerschmitt had taken his first steps in aviation, Friedrich Harth, died at the age of fifty-five. On a happier note, during this same year Messerschmitt was appointed to the board of directors of the Deutsche Forschungsanstalt für Luftfahrt eV., the German Institute for Aviation Research, on the recommendation of the then Generaloberst Göring.

7
1937-1938

1936 had brought Messerschmitt his first real victory, but the following year was to be one of multiple triumphs for him and his BFW.

Meanwhile, civil war was raging in Spain. The German Legion Condor, fighting alongside Franco's troops in Heinkel He 51 B fighters, discovered that these biplane fighters were no match for the Russian fighters used by the 'Reds'. Hurriedly, three Bf 109s of the Versuchsserie, the test series, were shipped out to Spain where they were used operationally for two months early in the year. In this way, the Bf 109 was the first of the modern monoplane fighters to see combat and, after some teething troubles had been smoothed out, was able to prove its superiority. After their experimental operational use, the 109s were returned to Messerschmitt for further testing, where allowance was made for the experience gathered in Spain. In the meantime, series production had already been started at Augsburg-Haunstetten, and by February the first machines were ready to be taken on charge by the Legion Condor and the Jagdgeschwader Richthofen[1].

The second prototype of Messerschmitt's other fighter, the Bf 110, had been delivered to Rechlin for further testing. Before the summer, the bomber development, the Bf 162, was flown for the first time. As the test programme for the Bf 110 had run smoothly, an initial small series was ordered, and instructions were given to prepare series production of the new type.

---

[1] This was the first fighter unit to be established when Germany began rearming; Hitler decreed that it should bear the name of Germany's most famous fighter pilot of the First World War, Manfred Freiherr von Richthofen.

A Bf 109 of the Richthofen Geschwader. The additional 'X' symbols on wings and fuselage are Luftwaffe war-games markings

On 16th June, Messerschmitt attended an important lecture given by Ernst Udet, now a Generalmajor and head of the RLM's Technisches Amt. Udet remarked on the hitherto subordinate role played by financial considerations when new aircraft were ordered, as initially the most important task had been to build a strong Luftwaffe as soon as possible. However, he firmly believed that the time had now come to start rationalizing the aircraft industry. It was now essential to: reduce the cost of developing new aircraft; standardize as many parts as possible; simplify the construction of aircraft; improve the manufacturing process; economize on new material; limit the number of alterations made to existing designs; improve communications so that experience could be shared between the various companies; and finally to increase exports of aircraft. He also gave reasons for the choice of the Bf 109 as the Luftwaffe's standard fighter; namely, its good piloting characteristics, the cheap construction method, the possibility of further development, and the fact that it incorporated the best possible solution to the positioning of the engine and other vital parts.

The aviation industry was now faced with the urgent task of increasing both its production capacity and its efficiency. Within the next nine months, all construction departments were to be reduced by 40 per cent, production was to be both simplified and standardized, and, above all, production costs had to come down. Without mentioning any names, Udet told how the Luftwaffe had had to pay 130,000 RM for a certain fighter, exclusive of engine, while a

The cockpit of a Bf 109 E

Photo: Abteilung der Militärflugplätze

D-IJHA, the Bf 109 V7 (seventh prototype) with a 'souped-up' engine, photographed at Zürich's Dübendorf international air display in 1937

foreign company had offered them a fighter, engine and all, for only 90,000 RM. He also spoke of the collaboration between the RLM and the German aviation industry which had run very smoothly, Messerschmitt's BFW included. Serious difficulties in this respect were to come later on, however. He finished his lecture by giving particular instances of quotations from aircraft companies which, in his opinion, had been far too high.

The Fourth International Flying Meeting, held at Dübendorf in Switzerland from 23rd July until 1st August, was to bring great success to Messerschmitt. Among the many German aircraft participating were two Bf 108s and no less than five Bf 109s. One 109, flown by Ernst Udet, had to make a forced landing because of engine trouble, but the others gained many victories. The Climb and Dive competition was won by Dip. Ing. Carl Francke, a test-pilot from the Erprobungsstelle, the test-centre at Rechlin. This was a speed test in which ten aircraft, representing five different nations, had to climb to a height of 3,000 m (9,850 ft) and then dive to cross the finishing line at a height of between 100 and 400 m (328 and 1,312 ft). Flying Bf 109 V13 D-IPKY, Francke reached 3,200 m (10,500 ft) in 1 minute 45 seconds and then dived to cross the finishing line at 150 m (492 ft) only 2 minutes 5 seconds after he had started. His climbing speed was approximately 33 metres per second (108 ft per sec) and during his dive he attained a speed of 600 km/h (373 mph). Second place was also obtained by a German pilot, Schürfeld, with a Henschel Hs 123, while third place went to a Czechoslovakian, Perina, with an Avia B 534, who dived with his engine wide

A Bf 109 B-1 with Schwarz fixed-pitch wooden propeller, photographed during manoeuvres held on 20th September 1937. The aircraft are ready for action against 'enemy' bombers

open. The speed event around a 50-km circuit, which had to be flown four times, was also won by Francke, flying Bf 109 V 8 D-IPLU, while second place was gained by Ch. Gardner in a Percival Mew Gull. The Alpenflug for single-engined aircraft was won by Major Seidemann, flying the same Bf 109, V 8 D-IPLU. This event was flown over a circuit of 367 km (228 miles) from Düben-dorf to Bellinzona and back, with landings at Thun and Bellinzona. Seide-mann's average speed was 387 km/h (240 mph), his flying time being something less than 57 minutes. Second place went to Lt. Haldo, a Czechoslovakian pilot flying an Avia B 534, who took more than 63 minutes to complete the circuit. The Alpenflug for teams of three aircraft, flown over the same circuit, was again won by three Bf 109s: V 8 (D-IPLU), V 9 and B 02 (D-IEKS), flown by Hauptmann Restemeier, and Oberleutnants Trautloft and Schleif.

All these victories caused quite a stir abroad, especially as the German Ministry of Propaganda had been claiming that the Bf 109 now equipped all German fighter units, which was far from the truth. The commotion within most European air forces was made worse by another German victory at Dübendorf, which proved that the Luftwaffe now had a bomber, the Dornier Do 17, faster than any fighter in service with any other air force.

Dr Hermann Wurster, Messerschmitt's chief test pilot from January 1936, in the record-breaking Bf 109 V13. This photograph of the V13 shows a complete absence of censorship of the reflector gun-sight which would have been in force in Britain up to and including the early war years 1939–40

The Bf 109's prestige was dramatically increased when, for the first time in history, a German pilot flying a German aircraft was able to break the absolute speed record for landplanes. His mount: Bf 109 V 13, D-IPKY. Following the extraordinary performance of the 109s at Dübendorf and the large orders that ensued, Messerschmitt's thoughts had turned towards the world speed record. D-IPKY was slightly altered. A new spinner and a more streamlined canopy were fitted, and all slits were taped over. The machine was polished to a high degree, and even the venturi tube was removed: the pilot, Wurster, would have to do without an airspeed indicator, and would be unable to use his flaps. A specially prepared Daimler-Benz DB 601 was installed. This could be revved up to 2,800 rpm, 600 more than usual, and delivered no less than 1,700 hp when run with special sparking-plugs, manufactured by Bosch, and special highly inflammable and poisonous fuel. It had a very high compression and could be run at full power for a short period only. It had to be warmed up with normal sparking-plugs, which then had to be replaced, all twenty-four of them, by the special plugs.

Flying along the 3-km (1·8 miles) measuring stretch, which ran parallel to the track of the Augsburg–Buchloe railway, Dr Wurster achieved a mean speed of 379 mph, thereby bettering by 65 mph the previous record set by Howard Hughes in his Hughes H 1, at Santa Ana, California, on Friday 13th September 1935.

Messerschmitt was constantly trying to improve the 109, and some time after the magnificent victories at Dübendorf he received an order for a small series of an improved version, the Bf 109 D. He was also working on the new Projekt 1059, with which he intended to break the absolute speed record, seaplanes included. The RLM ordered three machines of this type, which they designated

Gun-testing a Bf 109. The tripods and the bar running through the fuselage hold the aircraft in a horizontal position, while the ropes hold the fuselage steady as the guns are fired

A Bf 109 E-1, WL-IGKS, being tested in the wind tunnel at Adlershof

Shades of the American Gee Bee racers. Take one DB 601, build the smallest possible air-frame, add one pilot, and you get the Me 209 V1 (first prototype)

Me 209, as it was thought that the experience Messerschmitt gained with this project would be put to good use when designing other fighters. Another aircraft designed by Messerschmitt during the course of 1937 was the Me 261, this time intended to better long-distance records. As the next Olympics were to be held in Tokyo, it was planned that the Me 261 would fly the Olympic flame there, non-stop from Berlin. Adolf Hitler himself was very enthusiastic about this project, and so the Me 261 was unofficially referred to as the *Adolfine*.

The enormity of Hitler's rearmament programme was exemplified by the fact that in September Göring approved a procurement budget for the Luftwaffe, worked out by Milch, of no less than 3,000,000,000,000 RM. It became clear that some strategic raw materials would soon become very scarce. The orders given to BFW continued to increase, with the result that new buildings had to be erected continuously. Hangars 1 and 2 were enlarged, Hangars 3 and 4 were built from scratch, and a large new building was erected for the administrative and design departments. At the end of the year, series production of the Bf 108 was begun at the new Regensburg plant, which had been completed in an extremely short space of time. Erection had commenced on 24th July 1936, and the new plant was officially inaugurated on 20th March 1937. During his inauguration speech, Theo Croneiss violently attacked the Treaty of Versailles, which had proved to be such a serious blow to the advancement of aviation in Germany. This treaty had become something of an obsession with a large proportion of the German people, an obsession adroitly played upon by Hitler and his followers.

Despite the new buildings, BFW's production capacity was still too small to allow the company to fulfill the massive orders for the Bf 109. Thus, out of necessity, licence rights for this aircraft were sold to Fieseler, Focke-Wulf, and ERLA. Fieseler delivered the first Bf 109 B-2s, manufactured in Kassel, at the end of 1937, shortly followed by Focke-Wulf, who built Bf 109 C-1s at Bremen. Meanwhile, the ERLA-Maschinenwerke were completing production lines for the Bf 109 C. These were laid down in the company's modern factory at Heiterblick, 4 miles from Leipzig, which had been built in 1935 and financed by some Berlin banking houses. Before this, ERLA had manufactured small quantities of sports aircraft, but mainly Arado and Heinkel fighters under licence.

From a talented aircraft designer, opposed by many, Messerschmitt had now emerged as a true captain of industry, playing a vital role in Germany's rearmament and honoured on many occasions. He was named an Honorary Professor of the technical college at Munich, where he had obtained his diploma. He became a respected member of the Deutsche Akademie für Luftfahrtfor-

Interior of one of Messerschmitt's assembly halls. Note the sack of sand attached to the tailwheel of the nearest Bf 109 E, and the factory delivery code letters on the Bf 109s in the background

Bf 109 E-3 (W.Nr. 4101) spuriously coded '12+GH' at Biggin Hill, Kent, in 1960. This aircraft was built by ERLA Werke at Leipzig. It belonged to 2./J.G.51 and crash-landed at Manston in November 1940; the pilot was Leutnant Wolfgang Teumer

schung (the German Academy for Aviation Research), and even gave a remarkable lecture to this learned body on the development and improvement of aircraft performances. He was given the Goldener Ehrenring des Vereins Deutsche Ingenieure (the golden ring of honour of the German Association of Engineers); and the Lilienthal-Gesellschaft für Luftfahrtforschung, another association devoted to aviation research, granted him the Lilienthal-Gedenkmünze (the Lilienthal coin) for pioneering constructive performances of the first order. At the end of 1937, he was awarded the title of Wehrwirtschaftsführer, leader of the defence economy.

The enormous growth of the German aviation industry led to an increasingly urgent demand for more and more skilled workers. Because of this, Messerschmitt decided to establish his own training workshops, in order to train his own skilled workers.

The impoverished Germany of the twenties had now given way to a Germany which was, at least superficially, becoming ever more prosperous and, above all, very well organized. Nazi excesses were carefully camouflaged, in part so as not to interfere with the booming tourist trade. Many of these tourists made trips to the top of Germany's highest mountain, the Zugspitze, where they would sometimes see extremely fast aircraft looming up from the distance, to climb almost vertically into the sky just before they reached the peak. Indeed, when test-flying the Bf 109s, many BFW pilots flew the Augsburg–Zugspitze route, using excess speed to climb as high as possible when nearing the peak.

When the series production of the Bf 110 had only just got under way, the Luftwaffengeneralstab, the general staff of the Luftwaffe, asked Messerschmitt to develop a successor. It was not intended that production of the Bf 110 should be stopped, but rather that this type should eventually give way to a modernized version, incorporating more powerful engines and aerodynamic

A Bf 109 E, closing in at speed on the photographer's aircraft

improvements. However, Messerschmitt took advantage of this situation to start the design of a completely new aircraft, later designated the Me 210.

Early in the year, two first flights quickly followed each other. On 19th February 1938, the first prototype of the Bf 163, registered D-IUCY, at long last took to the air. This new liaison aircraft had been built by Weser-Flugzeugbau, after Dr Rohrbach had spent some time supervising the design. It turned out to be much more complicated and expensive than its rival, the Fieseler Storch, which had already gone into series production. The prototype made only a few test-flights and was then delivered to BFW at Augsburg, only to be given away to a technical college for use as didactic material.

A few weeks later came the first flight of the Bf 161, the reconnaissance version of the Bf 110. Neither this, nor the Bf 162, the bomber version of the

Bf 110, were to be taken into production, as it was planned to adapt the basic 110 for both bombing and reconnaissance missions. The first Bf 110 to be series-produced came off the production lines during July. Development of the Bf 109 continued meanwhile, and in fact during the summer a new version was tested, the Bf 109 E. On 1st August, Dr Ing. Wurster made an initial short test-flight with the record machine, the Bf 209. The aircraft turned out to have many short-comings and to be very difficult to handle.

While Messerschmitt was building the world's most advanced fighter aircraft, one of his earlier products, the M 18, was still going strong in Switzerland. An M 18 which had served with Ad Astra Aero, registered CH 191 (c/n 476) and had then been passed to Swissair to become HB-IME, had been put on floats by W. Farner Flugzeugbau at Grenchen, Switzerland. It made its first flight as a floatplane on 18th May 1938, taking off from the Bielersee.

The name Messerschmitt had by now become very well-known, both inside and outside Germany, and many people in high circles, especially Göebbels and Hess, wanted to see it replace the name of BFW. The BFW shareholders eagerly agreed to this, and on 11th July the firm was renamed Messerschmitt AG, while Willy Messerschmitt was appointed chairman of the board and general director. As all the Messerschmitt patents were still owned by Messerschmitt and Co,

Bf 110s flying in formation above the Alps. This is one of the many striking photographs taken by Messerschmitt AG's works photographer, Margarethe Thiel

were used to convince him of the might of the Luftwaffe and he returned to Paris very impressed by what he had seen, also informing the RAF of his impressions. This of course was the precise outcome sought by the Germans from the beginning.

On 15th October 1938, Göring gave Heinrich Koppenberg, General Director of the Junkers works, full powers to attain the planned production figures for the Junkers Ju 88. This caused some discontent among the leaders of the German aviation industry, as it meant that Koppenburg could commandeer labour and materials from competing companies, Messerschmitt AG included. As a result, production in these companies was seriously hampered in some cases.

On 18th October, Messerschmitt attended a dinner at the US Embassy in Berlin. The other guests included Charles Lindbergh, Göring, Milch, Udet, Heinkel and a number of ambassadors and attachés. The next day, he flew with Lindbergh to Augsburg, on board a Junkers Ju 52 3/m, to show him around his factories and to offer him two flights in a Bf 108. Lindbergh had wanted to fly a Bf 109, but at the time this proved impossible as the well-known French pilot Détroyat was also a guest of Messerschmitt's. If Lindbergh had been offered a flight in a Bf 109, the same gesture would have had to be made to Détroyat, and the Germans did not want the French pilot to fly their latest fighter. During the visit, Détroyat mentioned that French pilots fighting against Franco in Spain had tested a captured Bf 109, and that its top speed had proved to be only 465 km/h (290 mph). This caused an outburst of laughter from the

Photo: Messerschmitt AG

Dr Hermann Wurster shows Charles Lindbergh the controls of a Bf 108 during his visit to the Messerschmitt works in 1937

Germans. As usual, Lindbergh noted down his impressions in his diary when evening came. He wrote: '[Messerschmitt] is a young man, probably about forty and undoubtedly one of the best designers of airplanes in the world. He has a strong face and honest eyes. An interesting and likeable character.' Two days later, all the same, Lindbergh was able to fly a Bf 109, this time at the testing airfield of Rechlin. One of the first tangible results of the many visits paid by foreign representatives came in December, when ten Bf 109s were delivered to the Swiss Air Force, and thirty more were ordered. During most of these visits, the company's own photographer was present, Mrs Margaret Thiele, who also took many excellent air-to-air photographs of Messerschmitt aircraft.

Throughout 1938, the development of the Me 210, the Bf 110's potential successor, continued. Referring to this aircraft, on 20th September Göring ordered Udet to see to it 'that the heavy fighter could cover all of England'. War with England was no longer impossible, and the Luftwaffe had suddenly realized that most of its aircraft types were none too well suited to fighting such a war. Yet, at this time, no-one suspected that the Me 210 was to become a dismal and costly flop.

Around the end of the year, the design of another project that was to know many tribulations was taken in hand. This was Projekt 1065, later designated the Me 262. It was designed to be powered by a new and completely revolutionary kind of engine, the propellerless jet, which was being developed in

A Swiss Bf 109 on a cold winter's morning. It is equipped with the Jumo 210 Da engine of the Bf 109 B and the armament installation of the Bf 109 C-1

Photo: Abteilung der Militärflugplätze

secret. In order to keep drag to a minimum, a triangular section was chosen for the fuselage, rather broad at the base. The side of the fuselage and the upper side of the wing formed an obtuse angle so that no fillets had to be used, thereby reducing the drag.

1938 was the first year in which the Messerschmitt factories manufactured aircraft exclusively of their own design. The days of building aircraft designed by other companies under licence were now over; and in fact, the situation was reversed, as these other companies were now themselves building Messerschmitt types under licence. The new factory at Regensburg was now working to full capacity; 175 Bf 108 four-seaters were built there during 1938.

In the course of this year, Messerschmitt was awarded the honorary title of 'Dr Ing e.h.' (honorary doctor of engineering) by his old school, the technical college of Munich. The title was given to him for his outstanding contribution to the development of aircraft construction in Germany. His private address at this time was in Augsburg, at Gentnerstrasse 24.

8
1939

For some years, Dr Alexander Lippisch, one of the engineers of the Deutsches Forschungsanstalt für Segelflug (DFS), the German Research Faculty for Gliding, had been specializing in tailless rocket aircraft. On 2nd January 1939, after a fruitless attempt to collaborate with Heinkel, he joined Messerschmitt together with a team of twelve scientists. They formed the rather independent Abteilung L or Section L, and worked on a projected wooden tailless rocket aircraft, a successor to the DFS 194, which was designated the Me 163. Now that the Bf 163 had been abandoned, the number 163 was reallocated, in order to keep the project as secret as possible.

On 30th January, Messerschmitt, Heinkel, Porsche and Todt, who had all been awarded the National Prize for Science and the Arts the previous September, were received by Hitler at the Reichskanzlei, the State Chancellery. They were presented with the medal which commemorated this occasion, a medal with a diameter of 10 cm (4 in), suspended from a garland of 40 diamonds and a broad red and white collar.

With the Anschluss of 13th March 1938, Austria had become an integral part of Germany, and its production facilities were soon taken over for the German rearmament programme. At Wiener-Neustadt, an industrial town south of Vienna, the Wiener-Neustädter-Flugzeugwerke erected a new factory for the manufacture of Bf 109 fighters under licence. Messerschmitt transferred his own production of the Bf 109 from Augsburg to the new factory at Regensburg, as the Augsburg plant was now working to full capacity on the series production of the Bf 110. Before the end of the year, 537 Bf 110s would have already been

Enormous quantities of Bf 110s were built at Messerschmitt's Augsburg plant

built at Augsburg. In early summer, licence-production of the 110 was also taken in hand by Focke-Wulf and Gotha, so that even before the war Messerschmitt's two fighters, the Bf 109 and 110, were being built simultaneously in no less than eight factories.

Besides the actual construction of aircraft, Messerschmitt's sizeable Projektbüro kept on developing new types and improving existing aircraft. Early in the year, Messerschmitt submitted his Bf 109 T to the RLM. This was a 109 E adapted for use on board the two aircraft carriers, *Graf Zeppelin* and *Peter Strasser*, which had been ordered by the Kriegsmarine, the German Navy. An increased wingspan, catapult strongpoints, arrester hook and so on distinguished this type from the 109 E. During 1939, the RLM asked the German aircraft industry for proposals for an 'Amerika-Bomber', a four-engined bomber capable of attacking the USA from airfields inside Germany. Projects were tendered by Junkers, Focke-Wulf, and also by Messerschmitt, despite the fact that the RLM had decided that he should design and build fighters only. Messerschmitt proposed the Me 264, and his personal influence was such that he was not only allowed to go ahead with the design, but was also given an

A Bf 110 E-1/U2 of III./Z.G.1, carrying three crewmen

immediate order for three machines of this type.

Early in May, a cloak and dagger operation caused quite a commotion. Two brothers, employed by Messerschmitt as a pilot and a mechanic, who had both been bought by the French Secret Service, succeeded in taking off for France in a Bf 110. They had arranged to land the aircraft in a certain French airfield, the whole operation being carried out in total secrecy. But due to extremely adverse weather conditions, the aircraft crash-landed near Pontarlier, in France, killing its two occupants. Two months later, the Bf 110 was given back to Germany by the French authorities, but not before the Direction Technique de l'Armée de l'Air – who had concocted the whole affair – had examined the aircraft in minute detail.

Meanwhile, the development of Messerschmitt's first jet fighter, Project 1065, had advanced far enough for the final design to be submitted to the Technisches Amt of the RLM on 7th June. The twin jet was laid out as a super-fast fighter, and not as a bomber. Another project was progressing, albeit rather slowly: the Me 261, Hitler's *Adolfine*, construction having been started in the spring.

Since the day in November 1937 when a Bf 109 had broken the speed record for landplanes, both Messerschmitt and Heinkel had been trying to beat the absolute speed record. Since October 1934, this had been held by the Italian pilot, Francesco Agello, who had reached a speed of 709 km/h (440 mph), flying a Macchi-Castoldi MC 72 twin-float seaplane. Heinkel was the first to succeed: on 30th March 1939, twenty-two-year-old Hans Dieterle flew the Heinkel He 100 V8 at a speed of 746 km/h (463 mph). With this, Messerschmitt redoubled his efforts, and only five days later, on 4th April, Flugkapitän Fritz Wendel flew the second Me 209 prototype, D-IWAH, over the 100-km (62 miles) course. This 'vicious little brute', as he called it, had first been test-flown by Wurster on 6th February. The attempt ended in disaster. At a height of 3,000 m (9,840 ft), the engine suddenly stopped and oil covered the windscreen. Flying as slowly as possible, Wendel succeeded in coaxing the 209 into Augsburg airfield. 'It sank like a piano', he later recalled. Because of its very low speed, the aircraft started to porpoise on landing and eventually ground-looped. It had to be written off completely, but Messerschmitt was undaunted, and only increased his efforts further to win the record back from Heinkel.

The aversion of the two men for each other had by now reached monumental proportions. On the one side was the more experienced Heinkel, a cunning industrialist who had become one of Germany's most important aircraft producers before anyone had even heard of Messerschmitt. He was a good judge of men, and as a businessman had left no stone unturned to try to stem young Messerschmitt's rise. He was convinced that his fighter, the He 112, was markedly superior to Messerschmitt's Bf 109, and was embittered by the fact that his design had not been chosen for the Luftwaffe's standard fighter. He was now doing his utmost to ensure that the absolute speed record was held by a Heinkel design. On the other side was the young Professor Messerschmitt – now 41 years of age – who had just been named the Wissenschaftlicher Vizepräsident der Deutsche Akademie für Luftfahrtforschung (the vice-president of the academy for aviation research). A brilliant designer, he was primarily a scientist, inexperienced in managing an industrial concern, and undoubtedly angry at Heinkel's attempts to obstruct his progress.

The loss of the second Me 209 prototype was a heavy blow to Messerschmitt. As the third prototype was not yet ready, he had the special Daimler Benz engine that had been ordered for it installed in the first prototype, which had been modified in the meantime. This engine was capable of developing some 2,300 hp for several seconds. At last, after a spate of feverish activity, the re-engined machine was ready for an attempt on the record. But the weather proved most uncooperative, as it rained for days on end and the flight had to be postponed several times. Even when the weather improved the troubles were not over. The pilot, Fritz Wendel, was forced to return to the airfield several times when the engine over-heated. Another time, a piece of the engine cowling broke away, because of the shock caused by turbulence from a train passing

Photo: Messerschmitt AG

Prof. Messerschmitt is seen congratulating Fritz Wendel after he had broken the absolute speed record on 26th April 1939 in the Me 209 VI. The record was officially attributed to an Me 109 R – an entirely fictitious designation!

underneath! Yet again, a trim tab on the ailerons flew off, forcing Wendel to land the aircraft immediately. Finally, on 26th April, he was successful, attaining an average speed of 755 km/h (469 mph), 10 km more than the Heinkel. The absolute speed record had now been broken by two German aircraft in less than a month. The Messerschmitt record was especially played

The fuselage of the record-breaking Me 209 V1, D-INJR, as it looks today, stored at the Polish National Air Museum at Krakow

up by the German Ministry of Propaganda. Officially, it was declared that the record had been broken by an Me 109 R, a fictitious designation, giving the impression that the record machine was a 109 with slight modifications. Naturally, no mention was made of the fact that the life expectancy of the engine barely amounted to one hour, or that all the cooling water had evaporated after a flight of only half an hour.

On the same day that the record flight took place, the third prototype of the Me 209, D-IVFP, took to the air for the first time.

Heinkel still did not abandon the fight. The rules of the Fédération Aéro-nautique Internationale, the body sanctioning all aviation records, stipulated that any attempt on the absolute speed record had to be flown at less than 75 m (246 ft) above ground-level, but did not specify the height above sea-level. Heinkel's record flight had been at Oranienburg, some 50 m above sea-level, whereas at Augsburg Messerschmitt had had the benefit of a height of some 500 m above sea-level. The difference in air density had given the Me 209 an advantage of nearly 25 km/h. Heinkel's next step was clear: he would organize a new attempt at Lechfeld, in South Germany, which was situated almost as high as Augsburg. However, the RLM now intervened and forbade Heinkel any further attempts on the record. The RLM did not want the record broken by any other type of aircraft, now that it was generally believed to be held by the Luftwaffe's standard fighter. In fact the Me 209's record (for absolute speed for piston-engined aircraft) would not be surpassed for thirty years, until August 1969 when Darryl Greenamyer, a Lockheed test-pilot, flew his highly modified Grumman Bearcat across the Californian desert, at an average speed of 483 mph.

Record flying had now come to an end in Germany; all resources were to be directed henceforth to the production of warplanes. The enormous expansion of the German armament industry meant that strategic raw materials, already becoming scarce, could no longer be spared for the purposes of breaking records. Thus when the fourth prototype of the Me 209 made its first flight on 12th May, it was tested not as a record machine but as a potential armed fighter, which Messerschmitt hoped would one day succeed the Bf 109.

In April, Göring had ordered a demonstration of the Luftwaffe's strength, hoping to convince Hitler and his closest collaborators that more strategic raw materials should be allotted to the aviation industry. The demonstration took

Rearming a Bf 109 B-2. Note the VDM (US-licence from Hamilton Standard) variable-pitch propeller, and the Staffel insignia 'Bernburger Jäger' (The Hunter of Bernburg) of 1./J.G.137 behind the man sitting on the wing

place at Rechlin on 3rd July, and included among the exhibits a Bf 109 and a
Bf 110, both equipped with a newly developed cannon, the MK 101. Its most
important consequence was that from then on Hitler grossly overestimated the

This Bf 110 carries the symbol of the 'Holzschuh (Clog) Gruppe' of 11./Z.G.26, and also that of
the 'Pik-As' (Ace of Spades) of 5./Z.G.26 'Horst Wessel'. The ground crew is cleaning and rearming the 7.9-mm MG 17 machine-guns

Luftwaffe. All the latest technical developments shown to the Führer were for the most part experimental prototypes only, needing a great deal more development before they could be used at the front. However, taking them at face value, Hitler became rasher and rasher, until, on 1st September, he attacked Poland. Two days later, France and England declared war upon Germany. The Second World War had begun, barely twenty years after the end of the first.

The war had scarcely begun, when Dr Ing. Hermann Wurster made the first flight in the Me 210 prototype (registered D-AABF), destined to become the Bf 110's successor. For Messerschmitt, as for all other German aircraft manufacturers, this was the beginning of a hectic period: the RLM kept on asking for higher output, the Luftwaffe at the front for better aircraft. Both the Bf 109 and the Bf 110 were masters of the skies above Poland; their weak points had not yet been revealed. But that all was not well with the 109 was later proved by a complaint from the Chef für Flugsicherheit, the man in charge of flying safety. He claimed that during the year 1939 no fewer than 255 Bf 109s had been damaged during landing: the narrow landing gear was apparently taking its toll. When the RAF started dropping propaganda leaflets over Germany

In December 1939 (and not, as is sometimes stated, in April 1940), this Bf 109 E (W.Nr. 1231) of II./J.G.54 'Grünherz' (Green Heart) was shot down in France. It is seen here being scrutinized by a French officer and guarded by a member of the French territorial troops, armed with a Lebel rifle

referring to the 109 as the *Flutterschmitt*, the German Ministry of Propaganda countered the move by distributing more than twenty-five articles in one week, each one extolling the virtues of the 109. The Messerschmitt Projektbüro continued to develop eventual successors to the 109, and on 19th December, representatives of the RLM were shown the first mock-up of the Me 262. The first operational twin-jet in the world had already started taking shape.

With the advent of war, special precautions had to be taken when building new aircraft factories or adapting old ones, such as the construction of air-raid shelters and the dispersal of some operations. Naturally, this meant that additional, and considerable expenses were incurred by the aircraft companies. Negotiations between the RLM and the Ministry of Finance resulted in an agreement made in July, whereby these special investments could be depreciated forthwith. In this way, Messerschmitt AG was allowed to depreciate a sum of 7,000,000 RM immediately. Short term investment credits to the amount of 8,000,000 RM were transformed into a long term credit from the Bavarian Vereinsbank of Munich. The following year, the company was already able to pay back 5,000,000 RM, while the remainder of the credit was transformed into a mortgage, to be paid off within the next ten years. In the course of 1939,

The same aircraft on exhibition at an Avenue des Champs-Elysées department store. Among the personalities present at the inauguration of the exhibition were General Bouscat, representing the French Air Ministry, and Madame Guy La Chambre, wife of the Air Minister

Photo: via G. Van Acker

Bf 109 E-1s of 7./J.G.51 'Molders' ready for action during the 'Sitzkrieg' or 'Phoney War' in the winter of 1939–40

the capital of Messerschmitt GmbH, the company founded especially for the new Regensburg plant, was raised from 20,000 RM to 7,000,000 RM. A contract was also drawn up which made provision for the parent company, Messerschmitt AG, to buy the shares of Messerschmitt GmbH within the next ten years.

9
1940

The Bf 109 was still the mainstay of Messerschmitt's production activity, and early in 1940 development of an aerodynamically refined version, the Bf 109 F, was begun.

On 9th February, during a conference at his lavish country estate at Karinhall, Göring made public a decision which was to have dire results: all work on projects which could only materialize after the end of the war had to be stopped forthwith. As it was thought that the war would not last long, only those projects that would be completed in 1940 or come to fruition during 1941 could be continued, this policy being dictated by the scarcity of aluminium, iron, steel, fuel and manpower.

At this time, Messerschmitt's name was to be found everywhere, partly due to the efforts of the Ministry of Propaganda. He had to attend many social functions, give speeches, and write articles in numerous periodicals. He wrote one such article in February for *Front und Heimat (Front and Home)*, a newspaper for soldiers in Swabia. In this he recalled that when the Führer gave the order to rearm, his company was still very small and had yet to build a reputation for itself. Building the Bf 109 was beset with difficulties since at that time no-one in Germany had had experience in building warplanes, and it was essential to catch up on the lead shown by foreign powers. With deep satisfaction, he had seen the Bf 109 prove itself superior to any enemy aircraft, and had also seen the Bf 110 become the terror of the enemy. Hadn't thirty-six English aircraft been shot down recently, within the space of a few hours? 'We will fulfill the tasks put before us by the war, and will help our country as

Photo: US Air Force

The last view for many an Allied airman – a Bf 109 E attacking head-on. (But, with the wing radiator flaps in 'fully down' position, the 'enemy' is revealed as a captured 'Emil' posing for aircraft recognition training photos!)

A Bf 109 E roaring overhead

The aerodynamically refined Bf 109 F-o

the front expects us to.'

During the war, it became customary for military bands to give occasional concerts that were broadcast in factories involved in the war effort, during a special pause. These Werkspausenkonzerte played an important role in bolstering the German people's morale. Such a concert was given by a Luftwaffe choir on 13th March in the Messerschmitt factory at Augsburg, amidst machinery and half-finished aircraft. On this occasion, Messerschmitt broadcast a speech. He declared that he knew that many of his workers would rather be fighting at the front than working in a factory, but stressed the fact that it was their duty to manufacture the weapons needed by the soldiers. 'Where we perform our duty is decided by our Führer alone.'

Naturally, a great deal of correspondence was exchanged between Messerschmitt and the RLM. Some idea of the range of subjects covered by Messerschmitt in this correspondence, for the year 1940, is shown in the following resumé:

10th January: on payments received from the sale of licence rights

22nd January: to protest against Udet's decision that all research facilities should hand over 50 per cent of their skilled manpower

2nd February: on tests of swept-back wings, carried out at Göttingen

15th February: to refute the charge that he had paid extraordinarily high wages in order to lure engineers and technicians away from other companies. In his turn, he accused Heinkel and Junkers of enticing away some of his best assistants

19th February: to protest against the situation in which too many companies were building the same aircraft types, resulting in high costs and wastage. He claims that the German economy needs an additional half-million skilled workers

13th March: in response to the RLM's anger over the fact that Messerschmitt had given sub-orders to companies like Daimler-Benz, Drauz and Steyr, whilst aviation companies such as Weser were not fully occupied. He places full responsibility for this upon the RLM itself, accusing it in no uncertain terms of failing to plan ahead, causing delay in the procurement of aircraft and equipment

The Messerschmitt works in 1940. The Bf 110 is in for a major overhaul and engine change

19th March: on the use of steam-turbines to power aircraft

24th April: to refute the assertion that the Bf 110 equipped with a Dackel-bauch, a fuel tank under the fuselage, was not living up to expectations

23rd May: to complain that not enough steel was being delivered to his factories, and that he was losing many skilled workers, who were enlisting in the armed forces for a period of twelve years

7th July: to congratulate Udet on being awarded the Ritterkreuz des Eisernes Kreuzes, the Knight's Cross of the Iron Cross

13th September: to reassure Udet, who had telephoned him to ask why an Me 210 had had a tailplane failure. 'You have nothing to fear from the airframe.' He uses this occasion to remind Udet of his request for certain awards for some of his employees

14th November: to propose that Flugkapitän Fritz Wendel and Alois Sdzuy, a mechanic, should be awarded the Kriegsverdienstkreuz, the Cross for Merits of War, as they had risked both life and health to expedite the development of the Me 210. Wendel had made some risky test-flights to try out a strengthened tailplane, and had been forced to parachute to safety. Sdzuy had done all he could to recover a crashed 210, despite such

Construction of Bf 110 D-os in Regensburg. Note the Dackelbauch, a supplementary fuel tank carried below the fuselage, which had a capacity of 1,200 litres (264 Imp. gal.)

Bf 109 G-6 of J.G.53 'Pik-As' (Ace of Spades) with an Italian Macchi M.C. 202 Folgore (Thunder-bolt) above the Italian Alps

Photo: Bundesarchiv

cold weather that one of his legs became frost-bitten and had to be ampu-tated

The RLM, of course, sent equally varied letters to Messerschmitt. For example, on 28th February they wrote demanding that the straps used to fasten fuel tanks to airframes should no longer be made of aluminium but of webbed cloth. On 8th May, Göring wrote to thank Messerschmitt and his assistants for their delivery record over the past few months; they had not only delivered the Bf 109 in the exact quantities ordered, but had also met many demands for machines from units fighting at the front. In closing, Göring wrote: 'I expect that in the future you will always be able to master the situation to the advantage of the Luftwaffe, even when under enemy attack', as if he had a foreboding of bombings to come. On 28th August, Udet wrote to Messerschmitt to con-gratulate him on being awarded the Kriegsverdienstkreuz. Indeed, the Führer seemed very satisfied with his purveyor of fighter aircraft, having said many times that he possessed 'the brains of a genius'. Messerschmitt's company was even allowed to use the title 'Nationalsozialistischer Musterbetrieb' (Nazi model company), which was included in its letter-head.

When the matter was urgent, the RLM would resort to telegrams, as on 25th May when Udet ordered that the prescribed monthly production of Bf 110s should be met at any cost, even if it meant working through the night. On 11th June, Udet telephoned Messerschmitt to instruct him to equip 500 Bf 109s and

A Messerschmitt works-development 'Emil' – Bf 109 E-4 (W.Nr. 1361) – equipped with an SC 250 bomb, used for bombing trials in mid-1940

300 Bf 110s immediately with provision for carrying bombs. Those matters which could not be arranged by letter, telegram or telephone had to be discussed at the RLM. Thus, at half past two on 25th January, all high-ranking engineers in the aviation industry were summoned to room 3280 of the RLM, where they were instructed to use more steel and magnesium, as aluminium

A Bf 110 E-2 fighter bomber of II./Z.G.76 'Haifisch (Shark) Gruppe', with bomb racks under the wings as well as under the fuselage. Note the extended fuselage for carrying a dinghy

was becoming very scarce.

During another discussion at the RLM, on 7th May, Udet urged Messer-schmitt to expedite the Me 210 programme. He promised that Messerschmitt would receive all the engines he needed for the Me 261 in due course, but warned him not to apply for these too early. It had been discovered that certain aircraft companies were allowing engines to lie about unused for several months, a practice that could hardly be justified now that engines were in such short supply. At the same meeting it was agreed that a Bf 109 would be equipped with a dummy gun turret with two machine guns. This could be done very simply, as the contraption did not have to fly: it was to be used simply for Press photographs. Only the outline of the rudder was to be altered, so that the air-craft would not be recognizable as a normal Bf 109.

On 10th May, Germany invaded Belgium, Holland and Luxemburg, during an offensive that would also result in the fall of France. Messerschmitt fighters ruled the skies above Belgium and France, spreading terror as they machine-gunned the roads below. Meanwhile, on 15th May, a totally new and reworked blue-print for the twin-jet fighter, the Me 262, was submitted to the RLM. As the diameter of the engines had been increased, it was no longer possible to install the jets in the wing roots; they were now mounted in pods below the wings. Also in May, the Konstruktionsbüro (the construction department) of the Siebel company was placed entirely at Messerschmitt's disposal.

A Bf 110 pilot searching for ground targets above Belgium, during the attack in May 1940

Photo: Bundesarchiv

An Me 262 preserved in the USA, at the US Air Force Museum at Dayton, Ohio

Towards the end of the campaign in France, Bf 109s and Bf 110s were used as fighter bombers, and from July the Erprobungsgruppe 210, a special unit which tested new aircraft operationally, flew these aircraft in attacks against British shipping in the Channel. Development of the Bf 110's successor, the Me 210, continued but this type was to suffer never-ending teething troubles, one difficulty following another. Messerschmitt could only hope that his other new designs would not prove to be so troublesome. In August, he ordered the start of the actual construction of the first three Me 262 prototypes.

A Bf 109 E-4, used as a fighter-bomber, being bombed-up by means of a special trolley

The second prototype of the ill-fated Me 210. Note the rearward-firing gun barbettes. Fritz Wendel had to bale out of this aircraft when the starboard tailplane broke away during high-speed tests in September 1940

Shortly after the German victory in the west, still in July, Messerschmitt travelled through Belgium and France, visiting the aircraft factories captured by the Germans to see what equipment and machinery would be useful to the German aviation industry. Soon both industrial and scientific facilities were being used by the Germans, and in this way, still in July, a Bf 109 F was measured in the famous French wind-tunnel at Chalais-Meudon. Later, on 5th November, an exhibition was held at Rechlin for the benefit of German engineers and technicians, displaying foreign aircraft that had been captured in Norway, Belgium, Holland and France.

After its successful offensive in the west, Germany's next objective was to bring England to its knees. The first requisite was naturally the transportation of men and heavy military equipment to English soil, and for this purpose aircraft as well as landing craft were considered. This proposal was by no means new, for even in 1937, when landing gliders were being developed in Germany, Göring had asked Udet on 19th December to develop a large transport aircraft with landing and take-off characteristics similar to the then new Fieseler Storch. Messerschmitt himself had given some thought to the problem of transporting tanks across the Channel by air, and wrote to Udet on this subject on 4th October 1940. In this letter, which was insured for 1,100 RM, he said that if the planned invasion of England was indeed to take place the next spring, it was

Bf 109 Es flying off the English 'White Cliffs' coastline. The nearest aircraft is flown by the Gruppen TO (group technical officer) of an unidentified unit

crucially important that tanks should be positioned in the enemy's back the moment the planned sea and air landing took place. He had discussed the matter with Professor Georgii of the DFS, and proposed that the tanks should be equipped with special attachment points, to which wings and a fuselage tail with control surfaces could be fastened. These contraptions could be towed down the runway on two huge wheels mounted on a droppable axle, while landing would be effected on skids fastened under the tanks' tracks. Each monster would be towed by no less than four three-engined Junkers Ju 52/3ms. Thus, twelve engines with a total horsepower of nearly 10,000 hp would get each tank off the ground and tow it across the Channel to England! Messerschmitt assured Udet that a number of these craft could be ready within four months, and asked that, should any interest be expressed in his proposal, he be told the weights and measurements of the tanks and those of any other heavy equipment under consideration.

The RLM did not accept Messerschmitt's proposal. Instead, they gave him and the Junkers company an order to present a project by 1st November for a Grossraumlastensegler, a large-capacity transport-glider. All necessary raw materials and hardware for constructing 100 such gliders were to be ordered immediately. Messerschmitt's project was code-named 'Warschau-Sud' and the primary structure of both wings and fuselage was to be of welded steel tube,

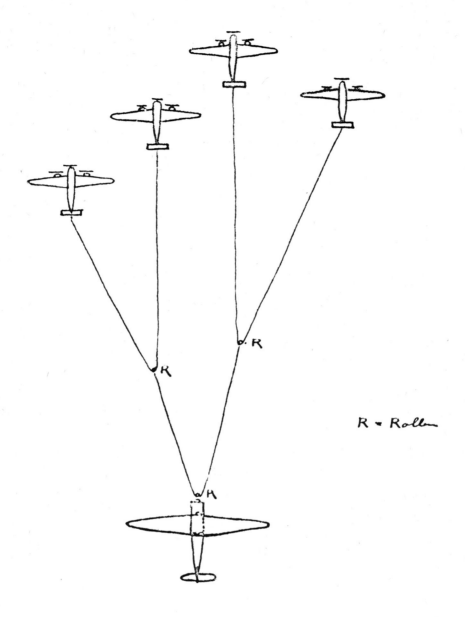

R = Rolle

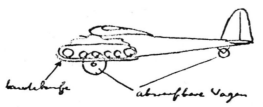

landekufe

abwerfbare Wagen

Mex 4. 1u. 40.

Imperial War Museum

Prof. Messerschmitt's own drawing, illustrating his proposal to use four Junkers 52/3ms to tow tanks equipped with wings and fuselage tails across the Channel. R-Rolle: pulley; Landekufe: landing skid; Abwerfbarer Wagen: droppable dolly

while the Junkers project, 'Warschau-Ost', was to be constructed in wood. Both designs were delivered in time, and a few days later both companies received an order to build 200 machines each. Messerschmitt's design was designated Me 263, although early in 1941 this was changed to Me 321. A special design bureau was set up at Leipheim under Ing. Fröhlich, and Messerschmitt put the construction of these enormous gliders in hand immediately. Construction of the steel-tube fuselages was farmed out to the Mannesmann factory, while the wooden parts were ordered from the May furniture manufacturers of Stuttgart.

The gigantic Me 321 A-1 glider. Tracked vehicles were sometimes used to tow it along the ground

While this new type was being taken into production, in November, the first Bf 109 Fs came off the assembly lines. But immediately, this type suffered some seemingly inexplicable and fatal accidents. After long and thorough investigations, it was discovered that under certain circumstances the hindmost part of the fuselage started fluttering, eventually breaking away. The 109 F was the first variant without tailplane struts, and this proved to be the cause of the accidents. The problem was finally solved by strengthening the fuselage on the outside.

During the year, Messerschmitt had begun yet another new design, the Me 309. A single-engined, single-seater fighter, this was intended to be the Bf 109's successor. In this design, Messerschmitt had taken into account all recent developments: by now, it had become clear that the development of the Me 209 was beset with insoluble problems, while on the other hand the Bf 109 had been faced with a direct competitor, the Focke-Wulf FW 190, of which a first series of forty machines had already been ordered.

During the autumn, an old acquaintance of Messerschmitt's frequently appeared in Augsburg – Rudolf Hess, the Führer's Stellvertreter, or Deputy. When war first broke out, Hess had been asked to promise Hitler that, for reasons of personal safety, he would not fly for its duration. He had made such a promise, but had set a time limit of one year only. When the first year had passed, and Hitler had probably forgotten the whole affair, he had asked Udet if he could try out some new aircraft. Udet had refused, and Hess turned to Messerschmitt. Initially, Messerschmitt refused as well, but when Hess told him that his position as Hitler's Deputy gave him the right to do so, Messerschmitt allowed him to test-fly some new Bf 110s at Augsburg. Despite his introvert character, the other Messerschmitt pilots regarded Hess as a good Flugkamerad, or flying buddy. After each flight, Hess would make some remark or other about the aircraft, and one day he told Messerschmitt that the Bf 110 was undoubtedly only suited to short flights, as it would lose its manoeuvrability if extra fuel tanks were installed. Immediately, Messerschmitt had two extra tanks installed, each with a capacity of 700 litres (154 imp gal) of fuel. Another time, Hess succeeded in having a more powerful wireless fitted. When Hess had flown the same Bf 110 more than twenty times, in order 'to relax', as he put it, various people started voicing their suspicions to Messerschmitt. Hess then began alluding to some official flight to Norway – no-one suspected his real intentions.

Two days before Christmas, the prototype of the Me 261, Hitler's *Adolfine*, made its first flight. All thoughts of it flying the Olympic flame to Tokyo were now abandoned, but it was planned that this type should carry out long-distance reconnaissance flights over the Atlantic.

Towards the end of the year, the RLM officials stationed at every Messerschmitt factory, and indeed at all other aviation plants, were instructed to ensure that nothing was scrapped which might be of possible interest to an aviation museum. All potential private collections also had to be reported. Messerschmitt himself had always shown a deep interest in any advance in the science of aeronautics, and did all he could to be kept informed of the latest developments. For example, when he heard about a report that the Italian company Caproni had developed an electro-magnetic device for increasing the speed of aircraft, he immediately asked the RLM for further information.

Two Bf 110 C-7s carrying two 500-kg (1,100-lb) bombs

However, in his reply of 11th May, the Luftwaffe's Chief-Engineer Lucht wrote that the device was believed to be simply a propaganda gimmick.

In order to obtain foreign currency, which Germany needed to be able to buy strategic raw materials abroad, a part of the production of Bf 109s was allowed to be exported, even in wartime. In 1940, 73 went to Yugoslavia, and 5 were even sold to the USSR, although an order for 40 from Hungary was not fulfilled to avoid antagonizing its neighbour, Romania. Even in 1939, the total value realized by Messerschmitt exports had amounted to 80,000,000 RM. The huge profits that were made allowed the Messerschmitt company to buy up other companies: in March, it had bought a factory at Kematen, in the Tyrol (formerly in Austria), and during the course of the year it acquired two further companies, Leichtbau GmbH of Regensburg, and Uher and Co of Munich. In the spring, the last Messerschmitt AG shares still held by the German Reich were bought back, so that the parent firm was once again completely privately owned.

10
1941

On 7th January, Messerschmitt wrote to Udet to tell him of the Me 261's first flight on 23rd December. He reported that the aircraft had a range of between 12,000 and 14,000 km (7,450 and 8,700 miles), and that this could be increased, through further development, to 20,000 km (12,425 miles). However, he remarked: 'We are already too late. The US already has a long-range bomber at its disposal.' In the same letter, Messerschmitt proposed that a special aircraft should be developed to tow the large landing gliders, now designated the Me 321, then under construction. Udet took up this proposal, and himself initiated the development of the Heinkel 111 Z (Zwilling–Twin) heavy glider tug, consisting of two Heinkel 111 Hs connected to each other by a mid section equipped with a fifth engine.

On 21st January, Messerschmitt visited Udet at Berlin, together with Croneiss. Despite the urgency of the Me 321 project, Udet declared that he would only decide whether the project should be continued or not after the first flight had been successfully completed. However, he agreed that some of these aircraft should be equipped with captured French engines, this type being designated the Me 323. He also agreed that Messerschmitt should go on developing the Me 261, the *Adolfine*, into an ultra-long-range reconnaissance aircraft. He insisted that the range had to be increased, and that the aircraft be equipped very simply.

Early in February, Göring awarded Messerschmitt the Kriegsverdienstkreuz 1° Klasse, a medal for merits of war. But only a few days later, an ominous telegram was delivered to Augsburg. Lucht, the Luftwaffe's Chief Engineer,

To tow the gigantic Me 321 glider into the air, the Heinkel He 111 Z-1 (Z-for-Zwilling or twins) was used, a brainchild of Ernst Udet. But an attempt to use the five-engined He 111 towing Me 321s to supply beleaguered German troops in Stalingrad failed completely

informed Messerschmitt that Feldmarschall Kesselring, commander of Luftflotte 2 stationed along the Channel, refused to use the new Bf 109 F any longer, because of the weakness of its tailplane. This was the start of a long series of clashes between those who made aircraft and those who had to fly them in combat.

In the meantime, the large Me 321 landing glider had been given the appropriate name of 'Gigant'. The first machine of this type made its first flight on 25th February, towed behind the four-engined Junkers Ju 90. As the Ju 90 had barely enough power to tow the glider, and the He 111 Z tug was not yet ready, the Troika-Schlepp (Triple-tow) was used for later take-offs. With this system, one Me 321 was towed by three Bf 110s, a difficult and extremely dangerous undertaking that caused plenty of accidents.

At the end of 1940, many Germans believed that the war was nearly won, and it is thus hardly surprising that aircraft production was somewhat slowed down. However, when an easy victory showed no signs of materializing, it was stepped up once more, and from February onwards the Bf 109 was also manufactured under licence by AGO Flugzeugwerke at Oschsersleben.

As before, Messerschmitt still found favour with Udet, who to a certain degree protected him from Milch. On 20th March, three days after a visit by Göring, Messerschmitt wrote: 'Dear Udet, I have been told that it is planned to develop

February 1941: Göring visits the Messerschmitt works. Messerschmitt is explaining some blueprints, while Udet, Bodenschatz and Hentzen look on

an aircraft especially for dropping leaflets over the USA.' He then went on to point out that he had at his disposal three Me 261s, that were being furbished as long-range reconnaissance aircraft. These machines could be ready for missions over the US within a few weeks, or, failing that, the motorized Me 321 gliders, the Me 323s, could be used, equipped with additional fuel tanks. He ended his letter by saying: 'I can easily carry out such special tasks, if only I could be sent some engineers, as I asked you some time ago.'

Barely two months after Kesselring had sent his telegram to Messerschmitt about the Bf 109 F, he sent a second one to Udet, on 4th April, enumerating no less than twenty-five complaints about this same type. Udet immediately sent a copy to Messerschmitt by telex, asking him to let him know his own opinion right away, in view of what Udet called the fight against insinuations against a new type of aircraft. Some of the points of which Kesselring complained were as follows:

Construction of the aft section of the fuselage was too weak
Positioning of the pilot's seat was too far forward. When wearing his full flying kit, a pilot could not move the stick back far enough, so that no

all had a very adverse influence upon Messerschmitt's prestige. Even his friend Udet, egged on by Milch, could no longer ignore the situation, and on 27th June he sent Messerschmitt a letter containing a series of reproaches. Bf 109s failed in flight, their landing gear broke on landing, and their wings became deformed. The Me 210's landing gear caused trouble and its rudder periodically broke loose. An Me 321 had crashed inexplicably, and so Udet went on, one reproach following another. His letter surprised and confused Messerschmitt, who waited some time before replying to each criticism in detail.

In his reply he pointed out that, apart for the Me 321 accident which was

From left to right: a sceptical Udet, an anxious Göring, and an amused Messerschmitt, watching a demonstration in 1941

caused entirely by exceptional weather conditions, nearly all these failures had been met at speeds of above 850 km/h (528 mph), and that not enough was known about the distribution of loads at very high speeds. He went on to say: 'My trade brings with it many anxieties. I could make matters much simpler for myself and only build aircraft which stayed within the sphere of our knowledge. Then nothing very much could go wrong, but this would mean that these aircraft would in no way be superior to others. I could also, as is often the case in technical matters, wait until the necessary research has been completed before I started building a new aircraft. If this were the case now, I would have to wait until a series of wind-tunnels had started operating, and until a number of tests had been made with high-speed aircraft by service pilots. You must agree that this responsibility cannot be undertaken, as the loss of time it would entail would be completely unacceptable. We must keep on taking risks, building aircraft which advance into unknown territories, and learning from the bitter losses in lives and materials. It is self-evident that the utmost care is taken, and that all unnecessary risks are avoided when experimenting. But who will set himself up as the judge after the event, and declare that "one should have known"?'

He continued: 'Unfortunately, I fear that this war will last for a long time yet. The American entry will shift the struggle even more towards the technical side. The Americans are both extraordinary producers and clever organizers. They have technical resources that we lack, and they also have a huge, and resilient fund of manpower. Their strategic position is much better than ours: they have bases all around us, from which they can send their bombs, and we have none close to them. The Luftwaffe alone can provide us with such bases. For this, very fast long-range aircraft are needed, to rule the seas, to destroy ships around the enemy's strongpoints, and transport aircraft to allow heavy loads to be landed at such strongpoints.

'The enemy will also build such aircraft. The enemy has long-range aircraft and we have none. A great deal has to be made up for. In order for us to obtain a technical lead, the following measures have to be taken: development of research stations at the expense of those companies which have contributed little, in order to speed up development; total reorganization of licence arrangements, so that series production can start sooner, with as little preparation as possible, thus saving highly qualified manpower for other uses.' Messerschmitt also proposed that collaboration between him and Udet should become much closer, to avoid such strains developing between them.

But his letter did not solve the problems surrounding the Me 210. The aircraft was still entering flat spins with no provocation, resulting in crashes in which even experienced test-pilots were killed. Scarcely a month after his first bitter letter, Udet once more wrote to Augsburg. 'Once again, we have received no Me 210s for battle tests this month, so that service use of this type has had to be postponed for another month. I also have the feeling that you have made far too many alterations since the first prototype was built. The prototype and the proposed series machines are so different from one another that the test results will be useless insofar as any practical aspect of the aircraft's behaviour in action is concerned. One thing, dear Messerschmitt, must be made clear between us, and that is that there must be no more losses of

Photo: Bundesarchiv

An Me 210 A-1 that was flown by the Erprobungsgruppe 210, a special unit which evaluated the Me 210 in actual combat conditions

machines in normal landings as a result of faulty landing gear: this can hardly be described as a technical novelty in aircraft. All these unnecessary vexations and the unbearable loss in time force me from now on to regard your new types from a more critical viewpoint.'

Messerschmitt himself had altered his engineer Waldemar Voigt's[1] initial design – in order to make the Me 210 lighter and faster, he had shortened the fuselage by approximately one yard, lightened the landing gear, and omitted the slats. But now he had no alternative but to build and deliver the aircraft, even though they still suffered from very bad handling characteristics, as radical and effective modifications would have entailed an unacceptable delay.

Despite the Me 210 setbacks, Messerschmitt kept on designing new fighter aircraft. In July, while the first two Me 163 rocket fighters underwent their first tests at Peenemünde, powered by their own rocket engines, a new project was begun at Augsburg, in collaboration with the DFS. This was Projekt 1079, later to be designated the Me 328. An inexpensive fighter, it was designed to be towed behind He 177 or Me 264 bombers, and cast off only when the bombers were attacked by enemy fighters. The aircraft was expendable: it was

[1] During the First World War, Ing. Waldemar Voigt had designed fighter aircraft together with Karl Theiss for the Halberstädter Flugzeugwerke GmbH at Halberstadt.

A visit by Adolf Hitler in person . . . Everything had to look spic and span, and you wore either a uniform or a decent dark suit with a Nazi party badge in the lapel. From left to right: Theo Croneiss, Prof. Messerschmitt, Adolf Hitler, F. Hentzen, and R. Kokothaki. Ernst Udet is on the far right in the third row

to be used only once, and was powered by two very simple and cheap Argus 014 intermittent propulsive (pulse-jet) ducts.

That security was now taken extremely seriously in Germany became apparent when a telephone scrambling device was fitted to Messerschmitt's telephone in Augsburg. When the 'secret' button was pushed, a green bulb started to burn and from then on any wiretapping was impossible.

On 7th August, Milch and Udet paid a visit to the Messerschmitt works, as they had become uneasy about the delay in supply of both the Bf 109 and the Me 210. When Messerschmitt showed Milch the Me 262, his reaction was icy-cold: he replied that he was not the slightest bit interested in this aircraft, but wanted to know when production of the Bf 109 F was going to get underway. He forbade any further work on the Me 262 until series production of the Bf 109 F was running smoothly. However, after the visit, Messerschmitt was able to persuade the RLM's permanent inspector to let him continue working on the Me 262. He also continued to work on the four-engined Me 264 bomber at Neu-Offing near Ulm.

Production of the large Me 321 landing gliders went ahead without any major problems, the hundredth machine being delivered during the summer. Design as well as production of this type had been carried out in record time. The collaboration between Messerschmitt and Lippisch was not so trouble-free, however, as these two talented designers had had many differences of opinion. Messerschmitt considered the Projektbüro Lippisch more as a rival than an actual part of his company. It had been planned for some time to move this Projektbüro to Obertraubling, but after an outspoken discussion between the two men it was decided that it should be kept at Augsburg. It was also agreed that more justice would be given to Lippisch's name, in connection with those aircraft designed by him. Messerschmitt accepted that the Projektbüro Lippisch should be considered as not subordinate to but on the same level as the Projektbüro Voigt where Messerschmitt's own designs were formulated. Both Büros were to have access, with equal rights, to the Konstruktionsbüro and the Versuchsbau, the experimental workshops.

Lippisch's work was soon to be crowned with spectacular success. On 2nd October, Heini Dittmar took off in an Me 163 A from Peenemünde airfield, towed by a Bf 110. At an altitude of 13,000 ft he cast loose and fired his rocket engine. The tailless aircraft shot forward, faster and faster, until suddenly, when the airspeed indicator showed more than 965 km/h (600 mph), it went into an uncontrollable dive. Dittmar was able to regain control by shutting down the engine. Compression problems had been run into for the first time. More important was the result shown by the extremely accurate measuring apparatus: 1,004 km/h (623.85 mph). For the first time in the history of mankind, man had travelled faster than 1,000 km/h. As development of the Me 163 had to be shrouded in secrecy, no announcement was made of this historic achievement, but Dittmar, the pilot, Lippisch, the designer, and Prof. Hellmuth Walter, the designer of the engine, were awarded the Lilienthal Diploma Award.

Messerschmitt test-pilots usually received a very handsome bonus for performing initial or dangerous test-flights in new aircraft types. An indication of the scale of these is shown by the amounts awarded by the Oberbayerische forschungsanstalt Oberammergau to Oberleutnant H. Peters in November 1944, for tests carried out in the Me 163 B at Brandis Airfield near Leipzig: 1,500 RM for three successful test-jettisons of the canopy (a total of seven were attempted); 6,000 RM for proving that the Me 163 B could withstand 6 g's in flight (in fact, 7.1 g's were attained at a speed of 650 km/h (404 mph) and 7.5 g/s at a speed of 890 km/h (553 mph)); and 1,500 RM for performing the first flight with an Me 163 equipped with a more powerful engine, the so-called Marschofentriebwerk. Most pilots carefully invested these sums in real-estate or businesses, such as breweries. In this way, they hoped to be able to reap the rewards for their bravery after the war was over. Heini Dittmar was unfortunate, however: he invested a large part of his earnings in Czechoslovakian currency,

An Me 163 B Komet at the Deutsches Museum, where it is now on display

with the result that most of his savings were lost to him at the end of the war.

Messerschmitt himself had little to do with the Me 163, and was now faced with serious competition to his own Bf 109, in the shape of the Focke-Wulf FW 190. The Fieseler assembly lines had already changed over from the Bf 109 to the new FW 190, and soon both Arado and AGO followed suit. On 21st October, before an audience of some two hundred industrialists gathered at the RLM, Milch announced Udet's latest aircraft production plans. Henceforth, three FW 190s were to be built for every Bf 109, whereas previously the ratio had been four Bf 109s to one FW 190. This was a heavy blow for Messerschmitt. But at Augsburg, the fight was not yet given up for lost, and Messerschmitt's financial director, Seiler, immediately started gathering the necessary information to prove that such a drastic switch-over would delay the fighter production programme for several months. At the same time, it became apparent that certain irregularities had taken place during the comparative testing of the Bf 109 and the FW 190. Five weeks later, Milch decided to reverse the decision and build more Bf 109s than FW 190s.

Udet had been kept in ignorance of the irregularities during the tests, and this rejection of his plan was yet another of Milch's many humiliations. He was now in an intolerable situation. An extraordinarily able pilot, now no longer allowed to fly himself, a man of many outstanding talents, now becoming more and more the scapegoat for the Luftwaffe's shortcomings and other people's mistakes, once a bohemian bon-vivant, now the victim of ruined health, unhappy in his role as Hitler's provider of warplanes, disliking Nazism, bothered by the Gestapo, caught in Milch's machinations, he could see no way out. On 17th November, he committed suicide. The failure of the Me 210 undoubtedly had a grave influence upon Udet's downfall. During the last months of his life, he had energetically fostered the development of the Me 163 rocket fighter, intending to start production on 1st December, but after his death Milch immediately gave the Me 163 a lower priority, so that construction of the new type advanced very slowly.

Six months after Germany had embarked upon a two-front war by attacking the USSR, on 12th December it declared war upon the USA. What both Messerschmitt and Udet had feared now became reality. The enormous industrial, not to mention military potential of the USA was now directed against Germany, and all hopes for a quick victory vanished completely.

Throughout 1941, there had been many attempts to solve the Me 210s problems. Even the Luftwaffe had tried to make the type operational by equipping five Me 210s with dual controls by Blohm und Voss. But nothing helped. At the end of the year it had become clear that the aircraft was completely useless. A commission formed by the RLM to investigate the situation even recommended that production of the type should cease forthwith, and all spare capacity be directed towards producing Bf 110s as fast as possible once more.

During the summer of 1941, Messerschmitt AG, together with the Seiler & Co banking house, bought the Eiso-Schrauben GmbH, and also obtained one fourth of the shares of the Ungarische Armaturenfabrik of Budapest, in Hungary. The capital of Messerschmitt AG was raised by 40 per cent, so that by the beginning of 1942 it amounted to 5,600,000 RM.

11
1942

Messerschmitt had never really accepted the RLM's decision, taken several years previously, that he was to build fighter aircraft only. He was also very anxious to build aircraft for which a ready market would exist after the war. In view of this, he developed, as a competitor to the Siebel Si 204, his Me 164, a fast communications aircraft capable of carrying eight passengers. As all production capacity was reserved, it proved impossible to build the new aircraft in Germany, and so in February Messerschmitt arranged for it to be built by the French Caudron company in occupied France. Naturally, the French were very loath to work for the Germans, and in fact they took so long over the prototype that further work on the project had to be dropped.

For construction of the Bf 108 four-seater, an agreement had been made with the French SNCAN factory. They kept on producing the type after its construction had been stopped at Regensburg. In 1942, they built 50 Bf 108s; in 1943, 108; and in 1944, 12. The same firm also developed the Bf 108 into the Me 208, with a tricycle landing gear. Only 2 Me 208s were built during the German occupation, but after the liberation the French continued to produce the type as the Nord 1101 Noralpha.

In Germany itself, production of the Bf 110 had been hurriedly resumed at both the Gotha and MIAG factories, because of the non-availability of the Me 210. At the same time, the design office at Augsburg began developing an improved version, the Bf 110 G, equipped with more powerful engines and suitable for a variety of tasks.

On 8th February, Hitler named Prof. Dr. Ing. Albert Speer his 'Minister of

A Bf 110 C-3 of Z.G.76 'Haifisch (Shark) Gruppe' protecting German shipping

Armaments and Ammunition', in succession to Dr Todt who had been killed in an accident. A few days later, Milch, who since the death of Udet had taken every decision relating to aircraft production, single-handed and uncontested, had to acknowledge his position as subordinate to that of Speer. Despite this, the two men got along with each very well, and Messerschmitt now received directions from Speer regularly. A few weeks later, another decision-maker joined Speer – Fritz Sauckel, Gauleiter of Thuringia since 1927 and an SS Obergruppenführer, whom Hitler had appointed Commissioner for the Employment of Labour on 21st March 1942. He was responsible for solving all the problems stemming from the scarcity of manpower, but it soon became apparent that this hard-boiled Nazi had no understanding of the special needs of the aircraft manufacturers.

On 25th March, Fritz Wendel carried out the first flight of the Me 262 twin-jet, now finally equipped with its two BMW jets. Fortunately, the piston engine had been left in the nose, for shortly after the Me 262 became airborne, both jets cut out and Wendel barely scraped back to the airfield. Both jet engines had to be taken back to the BMW works. Meanwhile, the first tests of the Me 323 had begun at Leipheim; the huge transport glider was equipped with four, and

Like some prehistoric monster lurching into the air, the Me 323 D-6 takes off

later with six, captured French engines.

On the last day of March, Messerschmitt put forward his final proposal concerning the Me 328, the small expendable fighter, which was to be powered by two intermittent propulsive ducts and towed behind large bombers. But the tragedy of the Me 210 had now reached its climax. On 9th March, Messerschmitt had been summoned by Göring, and had been obliged to admit that the Me 210 was not yet fit for use at the front. Without first telling Messerschmitt, Göring had then decided to put a complete stop to production of this aircraft, replacing it by increased output of the Bf 109 and Bf 110. When Messerschmitt promised Milch that he would deliver six improved Me 210s before 1st April, Milch had given him another chance. But he was unable to keep this promise, and on 14th April it was announced in public that the whole Me 210 programme was to be scrapped forthwith. This was an incredibly heavy blow to Messerschmitt, threatening the very existence of his company.

For months at a stretch, spare parts for the Me 210, manufactured by other companies, had been delivered daily. The production lines were completed and ready, hundreds of workmen stood waiting for the signal to start production, 370 Me 210s were half-finished, and parts and material for no less than 800 aircraft had been delivered. And now the whole programme had been called off! Immediately, an order went out stopping all further production of spare parts, but Messerschmitt was still obliged to pay for all those that had already been delivered, and to pay all costs incurred in setting up their production. The cancellation of the Me 210 programme cost the Messerschmitt company tens of millions of Reichsmarks, and all it could do was to stock the enormous quantities of spare parts and raw material in two large hangars at Gablingen airfield. The decision brought the entire Messerschmitt concern to the brink of disaster, and bereft the Luftwaffe of one thousand aircraft at a moment when they were in urgent demand. Ironically, this happened at the very moment when practically all the problems posed by the Me 210 had been solved. At the RLM, however, no-one believed Professor Messerschmitt any longer.

While the Bf 110's successor, the Me 210, had proved a failure, and the Bf 109's successor, the Me 309, was not yet ready, the first Bf 109 Gs came off the assembly lines. Some of these aircraft were equipped with wooden, rather than aluminium tailplanes. This change had been made because of the scarcity of aluminium, and also in order that a great deal of the work could be farmed out to smaller firms whose workers were not trained in metal production. In this way, it was intended to utilise the many skilled woodworkers in Germany, and more and more very small, even artisan companies now became involved in the German war effort. The wooden Bf 109 G tailplane provides a good example of how this policy was carried out in practice. It was calculated by Latvian engineers working in a section of the Espenlaub-Werke in Riga, while the actual construction took place at the factory in Nabern of the well-known pre-war glider pilot Wolf Hirth; an experimental all-wooden wing for the Bf 109 was also built here. The following year, the Schempp-Hirth company at Kirch-

Bf 109 G-10/V4 equipped with the so-called 'Galland hood' for improved visibility

Photo: Wolf Hirth via the author

Planing a Bf 109 G's wooden tailplane at the Wolf Hirth factory in Nabern/Teck in 1943

Photo: Wolf Hirth via the author

Production of Bf 109 G wooden tailplanes at Wolf Hirth's factory in June 1943

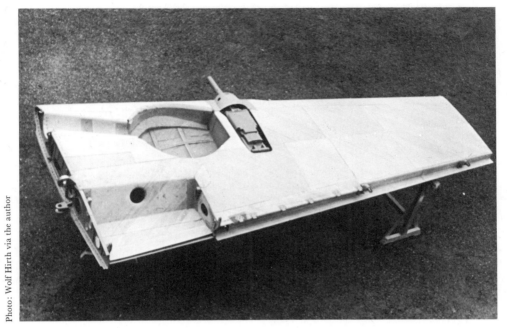

An experimental wooden wing for the Bf 109; only the fittings are made of metal. This project was also assigned to Messerschmitt's 1920s' glider associate, Wolf Hirth

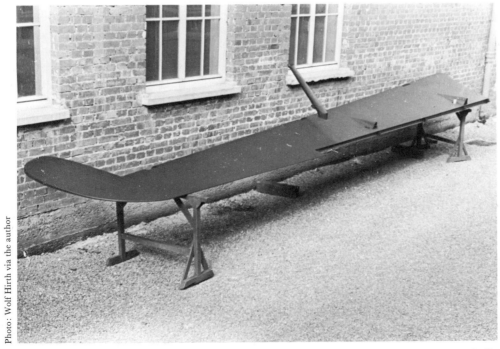

An Me 323 elevator outside the Schempp-Hirth factory at Kirchheim, where they were built under licence

Photo: Wolf Hirth via the author

Me 323 fins on a special trailer used to transport them from Kirchheim – where they were built by Schempp-Hirth – to Leipheim, where the giant aircraft were assembled

heim nearby, which had built the elegant Minimoa glider before the war, manufactured fabric-covered wooden tailplanes and rudders for the giant motorized Me 323.

It was hoped that such dispersal of aircraft production would make it less vulnerable to Allied attacks from the air, the possibility of such attacks being no longer purely theoretical, even in southern Germany. Indeed, on 17th April, just before dusk, eight RAF Lancasters streaked low over the roofs of Augsburg to drop their bombs on the MAN (Maschinenfabrik Augsburg-Nürnberg) factory where submarine engines were being built. Twelve Lancasters had left the airfields of Waddington and Woodhall to fly more than 500 miles at tree-top level over German occupied territory. Four aircraft were lost en route, and three more were shot down in the vicinity of Augsburg, only five returning safely to England. The MAN factory suffered heavy losses, but no-one at the Messerschmitt factory was unduly worried as it was thought that the RAF would not dare to return after such a high proportion of aircraft had been lost. In general, the people of southern Germany still considered themselves safe from aerial attack.

Messerschmitt himself was far more concerned about another enemy, namely Feldmarschall Milch. Shortly after he had cancelled the Me 210

Photo: Messerschmitt AG

During the summer of 1942, this Me 210 A-1 was tested with modified rear fuselage and wing slots

programme, Milch had also managed to persuade Göring to stop production of the Me 321 landing glider. When discussing this type, he had reputedly told Göring: 'This is all a swindle. During test flights of the type, thirty-six people have already lost their lives – the aircraft is badly built, and the steering forces are too high.' When, on 14th April, the Luftwaffe's Chief Engineer, Lucht, lamented the fact that Messerschmitt disturbed production by continually modifying his aircraft, Milch bluntly replied that he was seriously considering dismissing Messerschmit from his position as director of his company. He sent Lucht to Augsburg to investigate the situation, and at the same time told Seiler, Messerschmitt's deputy, that the Professor had to resign as Chairman and devote his time to research work only. Three days later, on 17th April, a memorable 'family' council was held. Accusations flew between Messerschmitt, Seiler and Croneiss, but eventually they decided that all they could do was to

View of the Me 210 A-2, showing the rearward-firing gun barbettes

try to make Milch change his mind. When Lucht arrived for his inspection on 19th April, there was tension in the air, and Lucht reported that Messerschmitt gave the impression of being a broken man.

Milch stuck to his decision. For Professor Messerschmitt, there was no other solution: he resigned as Chairman and Managing Director, and was replaced by Theo Croneiss, who until then had been Chairman of the Shareholders' Committee. Milch threatened to have the Messerschmitt factories run by a Kommissar if Croneiss and Seiler did not straighten out a number of abuses very quickly. Both men were of the opinion that all the problems posed by the Me 210 could now be solved at short notice, and put forward proposals in this respect to the RLM, promising to produce a useful aircraft. The loss of a thousand Me 210s, which they had counted upon, still weighed heavily upon the RLM and so they accepted the proposals eagerly. As the designation Me 210 had by now gained a bad reputation, it was decided that the improved version should be designated Me 410. Thus, after all, the Me 210 programme continued, under a new name.

But Milch had succeeded in depriving Messerschmitt of direct control of his company, where until now he had been the sole master. He was obliged to leave the daily management to others, and only in his Konstruktionsbüro could he remain his old self. He was always anxious to control and vet every detail of each blueprint. If necessary, he would correct calculations himself and often made improvements to drawings submitted by his engineers or draughtsmen. Sometimes, Messerschmitt would quietly place in their hands a new sketch or calculation, and frequently a designer, when proudly showing Messerschmitt his solution to a particular problem, would realize that in fact Messerschmitt had found a much better solution himself. When it came to technical problems, he would work on regardless of time.

Messerschmitt had placed a great deal of faith in the Bf 109's successor, the Me 309, which he hoped would be as successful as the former aircraft. The first prototype was completed in June, but the nose-wheel, at that time still a novelty in Germany, immediately started giving trouble. At long last, the aircraft made its first flight at Lechfeld on 18th July, flown by Karl Baur. Due to air-cooling difficulties, however, the flight only lasted seven minutes. The Me 309 was considerably faster than the Bf 109 and also had greater fire-power.

On the same day, Fritz Wendel made the first flight of the prototype Me 262, at Leipheim, now powered only by its two jets. This flight lasted for twelve minutes. The first prototype still had the normal landing gear with a tail wheel, and in order to get the aircraft airborne it proved necessary to brake slightly whilst running at full speed across the airfield; this caused the tail to lift a little, allowing the aircraft to take off with ease. A month later, the aircraft was written off during an attempt to ferry it to the Luftwaffe testing airfield at

Rechlin. In general, the future of the Me 262 looked very promising, but this did not stop Messerschmitt's Projektbüro from starting work on a new, and for that period very futuristic-looking fighter. This was Projekt 1101, a single-engined jet with swept-back wings. As the speed of aircraft increased, some hitherto unknown phenomena were manifesting themselves. These were the first effects of what was later to be called the sonic barrier, and the new concept of swept-back wings provided one solution to some of the resulting problems. Projekt 1101 was initiated by Messerschmitt on a private basis, for the purposes of research, without any order from the RLM. Meanwhile, delivery of the Bf 110s still continued, this type being used more and more as a night-fighter during the increasing number of night attacks by Allied air forces. The Bf 110 had not met with success as a heavy fighter, but now proved to be an excellent night-fighter. In July, the first Me 323 giant motorized gliders were delivered, having been assembled at Leipheim.

A night-fighter Geschwader Bf 110 E-2/U1 of 1./N.J.G.3 (coded L1+DH) on an airfield in Sicily, summer 1941. Note the portable gear for engine removal

One of the problems posed by the enormous size of the Me 323 was the height of the engines above the ground. Special scaffolding and ladders had to be used

The 'small' cockpit of the Me 323, seating the pilot . . .

Professor Messerschmitt was not completely ignored as an aviation industrialist. On 13th September, he was present at a speech given by Göring at the RLM, before a number of aircraft producers. Göring stressed the gravity of Germany's situation, and used the occasion to make some sarcastic remarks about both Messerschmitt and Heinkel. Aircraft producers were by no means having an easy time. Thousands of their skilled workers were being drafted to fight on the eastern front against the USSR, to be replaced by workers from occupied countries whom Sauckel's recruitment organization forced to come and work in Germany. Nearly all of them came with great reluctance, and acts of sabotage became more and more frequent. Some industrialists even went so far as to ask the SS to supply them with manpower from the concentration camps.

In the occupied countries, from whence the compulsory workers came, very few magazines were published: one of these was *Signal*, which was printed in several European languages and published in Berlin. Above all, it was an instrument of propaganda and in November it included a lengthy article entitled 'A Visit to the Flying Engineer', subtitled 'Inside Willy Messerschmitt's Factories'. Undoubtedly the article was aimed at making workers in the occupied countries less chary of coming to work in Germany. Alongside some photographs of Messerschmitt in the company of test-pilot Fritz Wendel

Photo: Bundesarchiv

. . . and co-pilot

A Bf 108 B used as a squadron 'hack' by III./J.G.77 at the Russian front in 1942. Standing in front of the aircraft is Hans Pichler, holder of the Knight's Cross, who eventually became a Russian prisoner-of-war after scoring 75 'kills'

and the German fighter-ace Marseille amongst others, the accompanying text told of the workers' swimming bath, the workers' solidarity, the cheerful and idyllic character of Bavaria where Messerschmitt's factories were situated, and the fact that practically no-one from northern Germany but only Bavarians were employed there. It described Messerschmitt as an ordinary man who, for the duration of the war, had given up using his own aeroplane and instead, like everybody else, travelled by train. There was even a photograph of Messerschmitt patiently queueing to buy his train ticket, while the text went so far as to describe him as a somewhat shy poet, who looked like a musician!

At the end of September, Messerschmitt revealed a new project, the Me 155. This was a fighter designed especially for use aboard the German aircraft carrier then under construction, the *Graf Zeppelin*, and in fact consisted of a Bf 109 G fuselage equipped with a totally new pair of wings. The project attracted no interest and so Messerschmitt developed it into a fast bomber, but as his design bureau was already overtaxed with work the project was later developed by Blohm und Voss under the designation BV 155. The Bf 109's planned successor, the Me 309, was demonstrated before Oberst Galland at Leipheim on 11th November, and was flown to Rechlin two weeks later. The second prototype was less lucky, as it was completely written off during its first

Oberleutnant H. J. Marseille, Staffelkapitän of 3./J.G.27, who on 2nd September 1942 made his 125th 'kill', and a few days later received the Knight's Cross with Oak-leaves Swords and Diamonds from the Führer in person. He is seen here while on a visit to the Messerschmitt works, in the company of Prof. Messerschmitt

flight at the end of November.

In October, the team of test-pilots trying to iron out the bugs of the Me 163 was augmented by a test-pilot from the Luftwaffe Testing Centre at Rechlin – a rather famous pilot, and a woman at that, Flugkapitän Hanna Reitsch. She

In August 1945, this Me 163 B-1a ('FE 495') was transferred to Freeman Field in Seymour, Indiana, along with 'FE 500', for use in a series of tests. Flying was to be carried out at the Muroc Flight Test Center (now Edwards Air Force Base). Since 'FE 495' was not in a flyable condition, it was never used for testing purposes and instead served in a USAF recruitment role during 1947–9, and was also shown at various public displays. This photograph shows 'FE 495' at a display of enemy aircraft near Washington DC. Regrettably, it was later scrapped along with four other Komets

had started her flying career as one of Wolf Hirth's most promising gliding students, and had later become a DFS test-pilot. Together with pilots Rudolf Opitz and Wolfgang Späte she started test-flying the first Me 163 B series machines, initially without an engine, being towed aloft by a Bf 110. Her fifth flight, however, nearly ended fatally. When she wanted to jettison the take-off trolley at a height of some 30 ft, the aircraft started to tremble. The tug aircraft alternately retracted and lowered its under-carriage, signalling that there was something wrong with the take-off trolley: in fact, it was stuck below the fuselage. Later she recalled, 'I had only one wish – to get to a safe altitude where I could find out if the machine could be flown safely.' Only when she reached cloud base, at around 3,500 m (11,500 ft) did she cast off. She was able to control the precious aircraft, but when she started to side-slip in order to get rid of some reserve altitude just before landing, the turbulence caused by the take-off trolley caused the aircraft to drop like a brick, crash landing short of the Obertraubling airfield, near Regensburg. Fräulein Reitsch sustained severe facial injuries, and had to remain in Bamberg hospital for more than five months. Before being helped from the crashed aircraft, and although she was bleeding profusely, she noted down a short report on the crash. A few days later, Hitler awarded her the Eisernes Kreuz 1° Klasse.

Messerschmitt's closest collaborator's at this time were Theo Croneiss, Rakan Kokothaki, Dipl. Ing. Hentzen and Regierungsbaumeister Krauss. But on 7th November, his friend and helper from the very start, Theo Croneiss, died after a short illness in Munich. He had been a Brigadeführer in the SS and had held several high offices. During the remembrance ceremony held in the large construction hall at Regensburg, Fritz Wächtler, Gauleiter of Bayreuth and an SS Gruppenführer, gave a speech, and Messerschmitt himself paid warm tribute to his friend who, always alive to the ideals of national socialism, he said, had been his company's leading member of staff.

The following month, on 8th December, Messerschmitt gave another speech during a German propaganda transmission destined to be broadcast abroad. He told his audience how he had started building gliders together with Harth, and had then progressed to building fast powered aircraft. He continued: 'The Americans have often broadcast and announced in the Press that they will gain supremacy in the air through mass production, but they forget that there is no reason why we Germans should not build our aircraft in large quantities too. There is one difference, however: our aircraft are technically superior to those

Photo: Messerschmitt AG

Prof. Willy Messerschmitt (right) with R. Kokothaki and F. Hentzen, his closest associates

of the English and the Americans, and we have at our disposal an enormous production potential in Europe, apart from the potential of our Japanese ally. Time will work for us.' In reality, Messerschmitt must have known perfectly well that shortages in raw materials had been creeping up for more than two years.

Also in December, the four-engined 'Amerika-Bomber', the Me 264, made its first flight. But in the meantime, Junkers had developed their Ju 390 and as this aircraft appeared to be better suited for attacks on the USA, Messerschmitt had to rework his own aircraft for use on extended-range maritime reconnaissance missions. In the same month, the first Me 410s came off the assembly lines, barely nine months after the entire Me 210 programme had been scrapped. As they were in fact simply fully developed Me 210s, Messerschmitt was able to use many of the spare parts and jigs that had been constructed for the Me 210.

The first prototype of the Me 264, completed late in 1942. Aircraft of this type might have bombed the USA. The cockpit is very similar to the Boeing B-29 Superfortress which flew for the first time during the autumn of 1942. The Germans had planned to bomb New York even during the First World War, and during the Second World War the Italians hoped that their Cant Z.511 four-motor floatplanes would carry out the same mission

In the course of the year only some thirty more Bf 109s were built than in 1941, namely 2,664. During the same year, Focke-Wulf built only 1,879 FW 190s, but this amounted to an increased output of 1,600 machines. Because of the Me 210 set-back, total turnover, which in 1941 had been 147,000,000 RM, fell to 102,000,000 RM, while the total number of employees fell from 15,000 to 12,800. In the course of the year, the factory at Obertraubling had become part of Messerschmitt GmbH at Regensburg.

12
1943

The Messerschmitt works were still short of labour. At the beginning of 1943, the SS proposed that 3,000 prisoners from the Dachau concentration camp should work at the Messerschmitt factory at Augsburg.

The Allied air forces were becoming increasingly audacious, with massive bombing raids taking place even in broad daylight. Many Germans realized that these attacks now represented a very serious menace, and so it was hardly surprising that the RLM decided to accelerate development of the Me 262, backing this up with the necessary orders. However, Messerschmitt preferred the Bf 109 to be replaced on the assembly lines by the Me 209. As an emergency solution, the Bf 109 was once more reworked, resulting in the Bf 109 H version, designed to operate at great heights.

The development of the expendable Me 328 was also taken more seriously now: it had been decided that the aircraft should be built entirely of wood, and to expedite production the wooden tailplane of the Bf 109 was simply taken over. The DFS built 3 prototypes and an order for 7 more was placed with the J. Schweyer Segelflugzeugbau at Mannheim whose gliders had, before the war, graced the skies above the Wasserkuppe Gliding Centre. Now, instead of graceful gliders, lethal warplanes were to be built.

On 5th February, Messerschmitt spoke over the German broadcasting system. Part of his speech was as follows: 'You know that for more than twenty years I have worked on the development of aircraft and you wonder why I still keep on working incessantly. I can only reply: work is no burden when we have found the right state of mind, when we see an objective before us. Today I

The crew of a Bf 110 G-2/R3 of Z.G.1 being given a jubilant welcome by ground personnel, after the Geschwader's 500th 'kill'

could not even live without working . . . I do not leave my work behind when I leave my office. Whether I am at home or walking amidst the mountains, my work never leaves me. On the contrary, I find new ideas when I am far away from the hustle and bustle of the factory . . . Work has become as necessary to me as daily bread. My mission is to contribute substantially to the development of aviation and, on a higher level, to the greatness of our Fatherland. We all serve a cause which is greater than is visible in our work. Even if we have to think in the first instance of the needs of the moment, something nobler always accompanies us: the belief in an eternal Germany, which remains the ultimate meaning of our labour.'

Messerschmitt's deep interest in long-term projects irritated many people at the RLM, and even Göebbels, Hitler's Minister of Propaganda, once jokingly said that at the Messerschmitt factories more work was being performed at the design bureaux than on the assembly lines. This was rather a strange remark from a Minister who, on 13th February in a fully packed Sportpalast in Berlin, had given the famous speech which he had worked upon all night, before a three-sided mirror: 'Do you want a total war?' he had screamed at his audience, whereupon thousands of voices had roared back a thundering 'Yes!' that was to be heard over radio across the whole of occupied Europe.

But to say that Messerschmitt's assembly lines were not turning out aircraft as fast as possible simply was not true. Besides huge deliveries to the Luftwaffe,

and Hitler's opinion of the Luftwaffe was sinking daily. Göring had suffered a serious loss in prestige, and now, for more than five hours, he heaped reproach upon reproach upon his guests. With considerable expertise, Messerschmitt tried to refute some of his accusations, but nothing could be done to calm the ranting, raving Commander in Chief of the Luftwaffe. Germany's 'total war' was going from bad to worse, one blow following another, and a way out of the desperate situation was frantically sought.

No-one talked about the Olympics any more, for which the Me 261, the *Adolfine*, had been built; not even on 16th April when Karl Baur, flying the third prototype, covered a distance of 4,500 km (2,796 miles) over a closed circuit in only ten hours. In peacetime, this flight could have been homologated as a record.

While development of the twin jet Me 262, called the Schwalbe (Swallow), went ahead at full speed, everything was made ready for starting production of the Me 209, the Bf 109's successor. A further version, the Me 209 H designed to operate at a high altitude, was already planned. Messerschmitt did not intend to start series production of the Me 262 either this year or the next: first, the Me 209 had to follow the Bf 109, and only then would the Me 262 be built in large quantities.

On 22nd April, the fighter ace Generalleutnant A. Galland came to Lechfeld to take a close look at the Me 262. He was very enthusiastic about the aircraft, but proposed some minor modifications, such as a nose-wheel and larger fuel-

An Me 262 A-1a which was shipped to the USA after the war. It was previously USAAF-coded 'FE 4012', but this was later changed to 'T2-4012'. When the trials had been completed, the aircraft was completely overhauled by the Hughes Aircraft Co. in February 1948. Note that the gun ports are sealed off

tanks. However, Messerschmitt proposed not to wait any longer, but to go ahead with a limited series, introducing the modifications while the aircraft was being built. Thus the Me 262's future looked bright. But this was not the case with another Messerschmitt product, the six-engined Me 323. On the same day as Galland's visit, 1,300 km (800 miles) south, 16 Me 323s of Transportgeschwader 5 were intercepted on their way to supply the Afrika-Korps. R.A.F. fighters shot down 14 out of the 16, and the slaughter was even recorded on film.

Collaboration between Messerschmitt and Dr Lippisch was proving more and more difficult. Messerschmitt had always looked upon Lippisch's Me 163 more or less as an unwanted child, but when on 1st May Lippisch finally left Augsburg for good to become the director of a Forschungsanstalt, a research establishment in Vienna, all further development of the Me 163 had to be taken over by the Messerschmitt company. On 22nd May, at Nabern, 100 km (60 miles) from Augsburg, a small glider which apparently had no connection with Messerschmitt made its first flight. At Wolf Hirth's factory, where wooden Bf 109 tailplanes were constructed, a special variant of the DFS Habicht (Hawk) glider had been built. The original Habicht had been designed in 1936 by Dipl. Ing. Hans Jacobs of the DFS, and was especially stressed to allow all manner of aerobatic figures to be performed. The span of this latest version was a diminutive 6 m (20 ft), and its extreme strength was proved by the fact

Photo: Bundesarchiv

Supplies being loaded from an Me 323 D-1 into a battle-weary Opel truck. As long as the huge transport aircraft remained balanced on its rear wheels, it was too tail-heavy to fly; a crude but effective control for weight balance

Photo: Wolf Hirth via the author

The Stummel-Habicht (Hawk) prototype in flight over Teck Castle in Würtemberg on 28th May 1943, six days after its first flight. Gliders such as this were used for simulating engine-off fast landings prior to flying the Me 163 rocket fighter

that speeds of 400 km/h (248 mph) could be attained. It was intended that it would be used to train pilots who had to fly the Me 163. They would first fly the 14-m version of the Habicht, then the 8-m version and finally the 6-m Stummel-Habicht, so that they would gradually become accustomed to higher forward and sinking speeds. A good exercise prior to flying the fast Me 163.

One month after his first visit, Galland returned to Lechfeld, this time to fly the Me 262 for himself. After the flight, he was wildly enthusiastic, telephoning Milch immediately to tell him that when one flew the Me 262 it was like 'being pushed by an angel'. He even suggested that all preparations for series production of the Me 209 – which he called 'a lame duck' – should be stopped immediately, so that the production capacity made available could be used to start production of a large quantity of Me 262s as soon as possible. In the meantime, other experts had denigrated the Me 209 to Milch, going so far as to assert that these aircraft could only be delivered by the end of the following year, and that their performance would show no significant superiority to that of the Bf 109 and the FW 190. Milch agreed that the Me 209 programme should be stopped altogether, and be replaced by that of the Me 262. Three days later, he even received Göring's consent. The decision was made known during a meeting at Berlin on 2nd June. Before the end of the year, Messerschmitt was to deliver the first one hundred Me 262s, and a special Kommissar was named for the new type: Oberst Petersen of the RLM. Messerschmitt did not agree with this decision. He certainly wished to build the Me 262, but thought it wrong to stop production of the Me 209 and Me 309. He was convinced that the Me 262 would fall victim to many problems once it started to be used operationally.

By this time, Hitler had grown very wary of the Luftwaffe's leaders. On 27th June, he summoned seven leading aircraft manufacturers to the Obersalzberg. Each had to see him alone, one by one, so that they could let him know their opinions freely, away from the influence of either Milch or Göring. Messerschmitt was with Hitler for a full hour, and used the opportunity to express his anxiety over the brusque switch from the Bf 109 to the Me 262. He also informed the RLM of his fears, and made it known that series production of the Me 209 was now ready to start. On 15th July, he proposed that series production of the Me 262 should be started the following year only, with production building up gradually to reach 60 aircraft by May. For this programme, he asked for 225 experts to be put at his disposal to build the necessary jigs, and for 47 draughtsmen to draw up the blueprints. The RLM promised 1,800 workmen to prepare series production of the Me 262, but they arrived so late that the jig and tool department lost more than 2,500,000 man-hours in nine months.

Then, suddenly, in early August, a Führerweisung arrived: an order from Hitler that series production of the Me 209 was not to be stopped!

Far from Germany, at the Conference of Casablanca in January, Roosevelt and Churchill had decided to try to get Germany to its knees by a combined bomber offensive. More and more Allied bombers were now appearing above Germany, but they were often grimly repulsed by German fighter aircraft, a deep thorn in the flesh of the Allies who had established the fact that 48 per cent of all German fighters were produced at Regensburg and Wiener-Neustadt. At Regensburg, however, most people did not really count on the possibility of a large-scale attack. This was despite the fact that on 5th April, US bombers had attacked the ERLA works, involved in Bf 109 production, near Antwerp in occupied Belgium. But then, Antwerp was so much closer to England than Regensburg, and the ERLA factory had scarcely been hit, although hundreds of Belgian civilians had been killed nearby. On 28th July, the Fieseler works at Kassel, where FW 190s were built, had also been attacked, but Kassel was not Regensburg or Wiener-Neustadt. . . .

And yet, in East Anglia, 525 miles from Regensburg and 725 miles from Wiener-Neustadt, in complete secrecy the 8th Army Air Force prepared a

Photo: via G. Van Acker

Bf 109 G-10 on an airfield in occupied Belgium

heavy blow. It was planned that Regensburg would be attacked from England, but that then, rather than returning over dangerous Germany, the bombers would turn southwards and fly to bases in North Africa. At the same time, Wiener-Neustadt would be attacked from North Africa, the bombers returning there after the attack.

The raid had to take place on 7th August, but as the weather above England precluded a mass take-off it was decided that the two operations would be effected independently of each other. At 1400 hours on 13th August, five groups of B 17s and B 24s of the 9th Air Force suddenly appeared above Wiener-Neustadt, having taken off 1,200 miles away at Benghazi in North Africa. The alarm had hardly been sounded when the first bombs were released . . . 187 tons altogether. 185 dead, 30 missing and 150 badly wounded lay beneath the debris of assembly halls, hangars and stores. There, where 270 Bf 109s had been built in July, only 184 would be completed in August. And not before October would the normal production level be regained. Of the many US bombers which had attacked, only three were lost. Now everyone at Augsburg and Regensburg was seized with alarm. No-one felt safe any longer. But it was too late to do anything about it. Barely four days later, on 17th August, it was the turn of the Messerschmitt factory at Regensburg to come under attack. Led by Colonel Lemay, the 4th Bombardment Wing came on, despite fierce resistance from the German fighters. The fighters succeeded in shooting down 17 Fortresses before the remainder saw Regensburg lying 18,000 ft beneath them, glinting in the sun on the bank of the Danube. After the attack, the American armada turned towards the south to fly across the Alps on its way

The attack on Regensburg: Boeing B-17 Fortresses drop their bombs on the Messerschmitt works

Four hours after the attack. Heavy damage has been inflicted throughout the Messerschmitt works. The airfield lies between the Danube (bottom right) and the factories. This photograph also shows the race track where Ernst Udet demonstrated the Flamingo prototype to the public for the first time, on 12th April 1925.

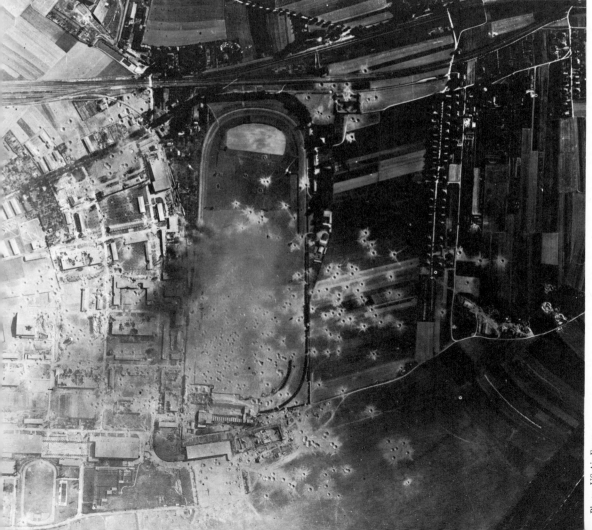

by a mid-section, but when the prototype was destroyed in an Allied bomb attack, the project was dropped.

The many obstacles to German aircraft production in 1943 are clearly revealed in the monthly reports that every factory had to send to the RLM. As an example of this, the reports of ERLA are shown below, a company that built Bf 109s in large quantities in the vicinity of Leipzig.

> March: 50 key personnel drafted into military service
> April: Deliveries of oleo struts behind schedule
> June: Insufficient assignment of foreign workers. Labour difficulties
> July: Deliveries by subcontractors behind schedule
> August: Deliveries by subcontractors even more behind schedule
> September: Deliveries of forgings and armaments behind schedule
> October: Difficulties with the procurement of machine tools, assembly fixtures and other equipment. Deliveries of armaments behind schedule
> November: The same difficulties as last month, plus shortage of light metals and labour
> December: Air raid on Leipzig. Transportation by rail blocked, trucks destroyed. Wing spar department bombed out. Lack of radio sets and tyres. One-third of the workers killed or absent. For planned expansion 1,700 men are required. In six months raw materials will be exhausted. Flight testing hampered by poor weather and air-raid alarms

And yet, around Christmas, the Messerschmitt Graphischer Büro, the graphics bureau, published a book containing cut-away drawings of the most important Messerschmitt types. It was meant to form the beginning of a published Messerschmitt archive. . . .

13
1944

Production of the all-wood tailless rocket fighter, the Me 163, had been undertaken by the Klemm works and not by a Messerschmitt plant. It was now slowly getting under way, and in the new year the first Me 163 fit for service use was delivered to the Erprobungskommando 16, a special unit which was to test the new fighter operationally from the airfield of Bad Zwischenahn. Meanwhile, it had transpired that the replacement of the landing gear by a landing skid imposed many disadvantages, and so Messerschmitt had designed a new version, the Me 163 D, equipped with a tricycle landing gear. Messerschmitt's design bureau was far too busy to cope with the new version, and so the RLM ordered that all further developments should be left to the Junkers company. After four prototypes had been ordered from the Focke-Achgelis company, Junkers developed the aircraft under the designation Ju 248.

On 20th February, the US Army Air Force started what it called 'Big Week'. The objective was to cripple the German aircraft industry by a number of heavy bombings carried out in quick succession. 'Big Week' began with an attack on the ERLA works at Leipzig, which had been attacked the night before by RAF bombers. Two days later followed a small-scale attack on Regensburg, and two days after this an attack on the Gotha-Werke where the Bf 110 was still being produced. The heaviest blow took place on 25th February, when for the first time Augsburg, and Regensburg also were attacked. In the course of 'Big Week' no less than 4,000 tons of bombs were dropped on 90 per cent of the factories comprising the German aircraft industry, and approximately 75 per cent of all the production facilities were destroyed. At Leipzig

The Me 163 Komet was the world's first rocket fighter, and a serious menace to the Allied air forces during the Second World War. This photograph shows Me 163 B V21 (twenty-first experimental/development aircraft) being tested operationally by Erprobungskommando 16 at Bad Zwischenahn during 1944

alone 350 Bf 109s were destroyed by bombs, while 150 were destroyed at Augsburg and Regensburg, and 200 at Wiener-Neustadt. Most attacks were carried out by between 400 and 500 heavy bombers. From now on, all the factories where Messerschmitt aircraft were being built would be bombed regularly, as indeed would the production facilities of most other companies. Halfway through March, Augsburg and Friedrichshafen came under attack; one month later, Augsburg and Lechfeld; in June, Leipzig, twice; in July, Regensburg and Leipheim; and so the attacks went on and on.

The Germans were perfectly aware that if the Allies succeeded in stopping the production of fighter aircraft, they would be able to bomb the whole of Germany systematically, as they pleased. Even now, the USAAF's attacks on industrial targets and the heavy RAF night attacks on many German cities had considerably hampered Germany's conduct of war. As a result of this menace, it was decided that an inter-ministerial Jägerstab or fighter staff should be set up, under the command of NSDAP member Dipl. Ing. Karl Otto Saur, whom Hitler in his will was to designate as Speer's successor. With the aim of increasing fighter production at any cost, one of its most important tasks was to get fighter production in full stride again at those factories which had been bombed. The 72-hour week was introduced throughout the aircraft industry and a special commissioner was appointed for every factory. From now on the management of German aircraft companies was practically taken over by these commissioners, the one appointed for the Messerschmitt works being Gauamtsleiter Professor Overlach. By taking a number of radical steps, eliminating certain production bottlenecks and using every possible reserve of the German aviation industry, the Jägerstab was indeed successful in increasing considerably the output of fighter aircraft.

One of the measures taken by the Jägerstab was the dispersal of the aviation industry, something which had been planned for a long time in order to make it less vulnerable to air attacks. Until then, all aircraft production in Germany had been concentrated into no more than thirty plants, but now this was to be spread over more than 700 different facilities. From now on, Germany's aircraft manufacturers were to go into hiding in woods and subterranean tunnels! Two completely bomb-proof factories were also planned: two large but low hills were to be built up with earth, and then covered with a 16- to 20-ft. layer of concrete; when all the earth was removed, the giant shells would provide factories of no less than 1,000,000 sq ft each, completely immune from any possible bomb damage. One of these factories was to be erected near Augsburg, for the purpose of building Me 262s. But the enormous amounts of concrete needed for these gigantic plants could no longer be realized in an already much weakened Germany. Instead, production of the Me 262, which was considered to be of the utmost importance, was to take place underground, in mines at Kahla and Kammsdorf and elsewhere. In these mines were assembled the sub-assemblies which had been produced in small plants scattered all over Germany. It goes without saying that this dispersal, and the setting up of subterranean production facilities, brought about many problems and difficulties.

Despite these, the first operational Me 262s were accepted by the Luftwaffe in April, and the first flight of the Me 328 expendable fighter prototype took place. Production of the Me 323 giant transports was stopped, however, after nearly 200 aircraft had been constructed.

During a meeting at the Obersalzberg on 23rd May, Hitler was told that no Me 262 bombers had as yet been built. He exploded with fury, and ordered that from that moment on, the Me 262 was to be considered solely as a bomber. A week later, Messerschmitt also attended a meeting at the Obersalzberg where Göring made the situation quite clear to him, and on 8th June a Führerbefehl, a direct order from the Führer, confirmed the decision. Some time later, on 6th July, the Me 262 V-12, a special version especially built for research work into high speeds in flight, attained a speed of 1,004 km/h (624 mph) during testing. Many influential Germans now tried to persuade Hitler to change his mind, but he stuck firmly to his decision that the Me 262 was to be built as a bomber only.

In July, both the RAF and the USAAF met the new German jets, the Me 163 and the Me 262, for the first time. On 25th July, an RAF Mosquito returned to England after a high-altitude reconnaissance mission in the vicinity of Munich with the news that it had been attacked by a very fast twin-jet; the Mosquito had been able to escape due to its ability to make turns with a smaller

Close-up of the Hirschgeweih ('antlers') of a Bf 110 G-4 radar-equipped night-fighter

abandoned as scarcity of raw materials now rendered construction of this large aircraft impossible. It had been intended to use the prototype to test steam-turbines especially built to power aircraft, but the prototype was destroyed during an Allied air attack. The Me 328 expendable fighter programme was also scrapped, even though Messerschmitt had put forward many versions; it appeared that the use of pulse-jets for fighter aircraft had many drawbacks. Saur, the leader of the Jägerstab, had hoped to be able to produce pulse-jet powered fighters quickly and in large quantities, but this hope, like so many other last-ditch German plans, proved to be in vain.

Since June, all aircraft production had been overseen by Minister Speer, under whom Saur had gained more and more power. This had been increased all the more by Milch's fall from favour. On 23rd May, Hitler had severely upbraided Milch for disobeying the order to build the Me 262 as a bomber. At this, Milch had lost his temper and cried out: 'Any small child could see that this is no bomber but a fighter.' He had fallen into disgrace with Hitler, and been sacked as Generalluftzeugmeister. The figures Speer's office gave for aircraft production were often rosily optimistic. Indeed, during November, Göebbels, the Minister of Propaganda, complained bitterly that there were striking differences between the fighter-production figures he obtained from Messerschmitt and those he got from Speer. Speer replied that many difficulties

An Me 262 B-1a (W.Nr. 110639) on display after the war at Willow Grove NAS, Penn. Before being painted in spurious markings as shown in the photograph, it sported the designation 'FE-610' and was used for trials with its Lichtenstein SN-2 (FuG 220) intercept-radar and Hirschgeweih antennas fitted. Sadly, when the trials were completed, the Hirschgeweih ('antlers') array was removed

had just been overcome, and that he could now tell the German people that the Luftwaffe would have regained the initiative by Christmas. Göebbels did not share Speer's optimism, however.

The latest version of the Bf 109, still the Luftwaffe's standard fighter, came off the assembly lines in September. These Bf 109 Ks had been built according to instructions from the Jägerstab, who intended that this version should replace the various versions of the Bf 109 then being built at several different places. Amongst these was the Köbanya Brewery in Budapest, where one Bf 109 G was produced every day in shell-proof beer cellars.

Although the Bf 109 was still Germany's standard fighter, more and more jets were now being used against the Allied bombers. On 1st September, General Spaatz, commanding the US strategic bombers, declared that the deadly German jets might possibly inflict prohibitively high losses in the near future. Under these circumstances, the RLM asked several companies to design a single-jet fighter with an even better performance than the Me 262. In response to this request, Messerschmitt proposed his Projekt P 1101, the single-seat fighter with swept-back wings, of an extremely advanced and revolutionary design, which his Projektbüro had been working on for two years. The RLM immediately ordered one prototype.

Then, on 4th November, Hitler at last gave his consent to building the Me 262 as a fighter, although he insisted that the aircraft be capable of carrying two 250-kg (551-lb) bombs if need be. The Luftwaffe could have had the Me 262 considerably earlier if Hitler had been prepared to consider the type as a pure fighter, but now the supply of the jet engines formed a bottleneck in production, as Junkers were at first unable to supply the engines in large quantities. During October, on the recommendation of Göring and Speer, Hitler awarded the Ritterkreuz zum Kriegsverdienstkreuz for war efforts to Professor Messerschmitt and Dr Lippisch.

The RLM decided to stop the development of Projekt 1101 in December, as in the meantime they had been presented with other projects which seemed to offer better possibilities. The actual construction of the prototype at Oberammergau was very well advanced, and so Messerschmitt decided to continue work on the project for experimental purposes.

Towards the end of the year it was decided that Junkers' development of the Me 263, the Me 163 extrapolation with retractable landing gear, should be accelerated at all costs. Work on the Me 163 was now being carried out even in Japan. At the beginning of the year, the Japanese Government had bought the licence rights to the Me 163 B and the Walter HWK 509A rocket engine which powered it. A finished Me 163, together with a complete set of blueprints, had been sent to Japan, but the submarine transporting them from Germany had been lost en route. The Mitsubishi company then started drawing up new blueprints following an Me 163 handbook.

As a counter-measure to the intensifying Allied bombings upon industrial sites and cities, Germany now developed a new weapon, the anti-aircraft rocket. The hyper-modern technology of this naturally fascinated Messerschmitt, and, based on the Me 163, he had such a rocket developed by a subordinate company, the Oberbayerische Forschungsanstalt Dr. Konrad at Oberammergau. In this way, a wooden, pilotless, tailless aircraft, powered by a liquid rocket, took shape. Called the Enzian, this missile was designed to fly towards the enemy aircraft at a speed of 920 km/h (572 mph) carrying an explosive charge of 500 kg (1,100 lb), and initially controlled from the ground. When it arrived in proximity to the enemy aircraft, an accoustic or infra-red sensor would take over control. Series production of this lethal weapon, capable of destroying enemy bombers flying as high as 13,500 m (44,300 ft), was planned to begin in May 1945, but once again the Germans were too late.

The dispersal of the aircraft industry brought about many problems. Foremost amongst these was a decrease in production, which had now become

Messerschmitt AG's plant in the Austrian Alps at Kematen. This plant had a large underground section, consisting of tunnels dug into the side of the mountain

totally dependent upon transport at a time when scarcity of fuel and incessant air attacks heavily taxed all forms of transport in Germany. By the end of the year, the dispersal was for all practical purposes completed, and production was taking place more and more frequently in underground workshops and small barracks hidden in the woods. The Messerschmitt factory at Kematen near Innsbruck, which had a total area of 85,000 sq ft, was now connected to an underground factory, consisting of eight tunnels hewn out of the mountainside, while near Augsburg four factories had been built under the woods at Burgau, Reidheim, Leipheim and Schwäbisch-Hall.

Once again, the monthly reports of ERLA for 1944 give an idea of the terrible strain under which the German aviation industry had to operate:

> January: Short of machine tools, spare parts, 2,000 workmen, and transportation as a result of the December raids
> February: Bad weather, air raids
> March: Air raids, many difficulties brought about by the dispersal. Insufficient replacement of destroyed machine tools
> April: The same problems as last month, plus labour shortage
> May: Insufficient deliveries of spare parts and instruments
> June: Deliveries of machine tools behind schedule. Lack of jigs and experienced tool-makers
> July: Lack of fuel for trucks, still lacking tool-makers
> August: Lack of equipment for dispersal and expansion. Lack of skilled workers for tool room and flight-test department
> September: No specific difficulties
> October: Delivery of engines and tail skids behind schedule
> November: Errors in wiring and instruments which were not discovered until test flights

And yet, notwithstanding the turmoil, tradition and folklore retained their place. On 12th June, Franz Hofer, Gauleiter of Tirol-Vorarlberg and an NSKK Obergruppenführer, wrote to invite Messerschmitt to the 7th Tiroler Landesschiessen at Innsbruck, on 1st and 2nd July. This was a typical Schützenfest, a festive occasion organized by shooting associations in which groups from all over Germany participated, dressed in their traditional costumes. Due to pressure of work, Messerschmitt was unable to attend. As always, he was obsessed by the desire to make his aircraft go faster and faster. At the end of the year, he proposed to make the fittings used to carry bombs underneath the Me 262 jettisonable, so that after dropping its bombs the aircraft would once again be perfectly streamlined and thus faster.

14
1945

The management of the Messerschmitt company was now unable to take practically any decisions for itself: all orders emanated directly from the Speer Ministry and from the various commissioners. There was a special commissioner and a sponsor for each type produced, and this situation was made even more complicated when on 1st February Herr Degenkolb was appointed general trustee for the company. Although the Jägerstab had initially obtained good results, it now became a great deal less efficient when it was forced to take the entire German aviation industry, rather than fighter production only, under its wing. When the Messerschmitt company proved incapable of meeting some of the demands put before it, the Speer Ministry had promised to get things done – but these promises could not be kept. Consequently, production did not come up to Saur's expectations and the blame for this was put squarely upon the Messerschmitt company, as no-one from the Speer Ministry was prepared to admit responsibility. Saur would not even allow these problems to be discussed: he simply claimed that the ministry had done everything possible. The special sponsors, trustees and commissioners created a mix-up in command responsibilities which threatened to destroy the company's own organization. Many of the personnel on Saur's staff had no knowledge of the special needs of the aviation industry, but this did not stop Saur from making promise after promise which simply could not be kept.

The transportation problem was now worsening daily. More and more trucks were needed to bring sub-assemblies to assembly facilities, to transport spare parts, instruments and so on, while the shortage of fuel became more critical day by day. Transport was taxed even further by the steady advance of the Allied troops. Production facilities and spare parts had to be withdrawn as the Allies approached, and yet the Speer Ministry continually demanded that transfer of plants and the like had to be effected without any loss in production. At the end of February, even Saur was unable to keep up with the demands of his superiors, and he was replaced by SS Obergruppenführer Kammler.

Development of Projekt 1101 still continued at Oberammergau, albeit at a slower pace. It was decided that the prototype should be built in such a way that the wings could be set in three different positions of sweep-back, as Professor Messerschmitt hoped to gain experience in high-speed flight, speeds in the vicinity of the speed of sound being envisaged. During a meeting between Speer and Hitler on 14th February, Hitler once more stressed the importance of the Me 262 to Germany's conduct of war. He welcomed Degenkolb's appointment as special commissioner to the Messerschmitt company as Degenkolb had previously obtained good results in increasing the production of locomotives.

A year after operation 'Big Week', the US bombers began operation 'Clarion', an all-out attack upon German transportation facilities. Even the smallest communications centres were attacked in the hope that the entire transport system, already badly stricken, would collapse and come to a complete halt. On 22nd February, an attack was made on Bamberg, where Messerschmitt had taken his first steps in aviation with Harth. Attacks by armadas of 1,000 bombers had by now become commonplace, and the reaction of even the

When the Bell X-5 made its first flight on 20th June 1951, it owed its existence to Messerschmitt's P 1101 project, conceived in Bavaria in 1942

German anti-aircraft guns was now weakened through lack of ammunition.

In order that special targets at least could be defended, work had started at the beginning of the year on a Heimatschützer or Home-defender version of the Me 262. This was equipped with take-off rockets to enable the aircraft to reach a great altitude in the shortest possible time. In this way, it was hoped that enemy bombers could be attacked at the last possible moment, when they had nearly reached their target. When the Me 262 Heimatschützer made its first flight in March, it reached a height of 7,600 m (25,000 ft) in one and a half minutes.

While the last Bf 110 to be built left the assembly lines in March, production of the Me 262 started in the forest plant at Horgau, some eight miles from Augsburg, alongside the autobahn between Ulm and Augsburg. The plant consisted of twenty-one wooden barracks hidden in a dense pine wood, invisible from the road or from the air. It had not been easy to find such an ideal location, in view of the many factors which had to be taken into account, such as availability of power and water supplies, proximity to a railway line, and accessibility to other production complexes. The woods had to be evergreen because of camouflage requirements in winter, and the factory had to be built without altering the appearance of the forest in aerial photographs. The complete factory had been built by 80 men in about six months, and when it was finished 850 workers could turn out 250 Me 262 wings per month. Working in the forest factories proved to be far healthier than in the underground factories such as Kematen, where 729 men worked underground beneath the surface plant which employed 2,302. The underground workers frequently complained of headaches, although their situation was a great deal better than that of some of their fellows, who built aircraft in some abandoned salt-mines. Here, tools and machinery became seriously corroded after only a few weeks.

From March, regular production was no longer possible: the numerous transfers and dispersal measures more or less reduced the Messerschmitt concern to a transportation firm. And yet, notwithstanding these nearly unsurmountable problems, no fewer than 1,443 Me 262s were built between March 1944 and 20th April 1945, 865 of these during the first four months of 1945. Everyone employed at the Messerschmitt works toiled for 70 hours every week.

Early in the year, General Galland had formed Jagdverband 44, which comprised the best fighter pilots of the Luftwaffe and was equipped with Me 262s. During the last days of March, the unit operated regularly from Munich-Riem airfield. It was an elite group, equipped with the best possible machinery, and yet it could not prevent the Allied air forces from dominating the skies above Germany.

The German ground transport system had now practically ground to a halt.

Photo: via H. Thiele

The same Me 262 A-2a in a line-up of captured German and Japanese aircraft at Wright Field, Dayton, Ohio. It was used by USAAF test-pilots for high-speed tests and had its guns removed and its gun ports sealed off

said, since Germany had already carried out this policy in the case of Rome and Florence, amongst other cities, and he stressed the fact that Germany, and not her enemies, would be charged by the civilised world should it be destroyed. On 11th April, he wrote to Gauleiter Wächtler, presenting the same argument.

At the end of April, Allied troops invaded Bavaria, and huge quantities of documents and photographs from the Messerschmitt archives were burned. Some blueprints were placed in containers and hidden under the ground or in caves, but most of these were soon found by the Allied troops. Some fell into the

The end of the Messerschmitt empire. This photograph shows the final assembly hall of the ERLA factory at Leipzig-Heiterblick. The ERLA complex comprised 18 dispersal plants, 13 component plants, and 5 final assembly plants. It produced some 32 per cent of all Bf 109s built in Germany

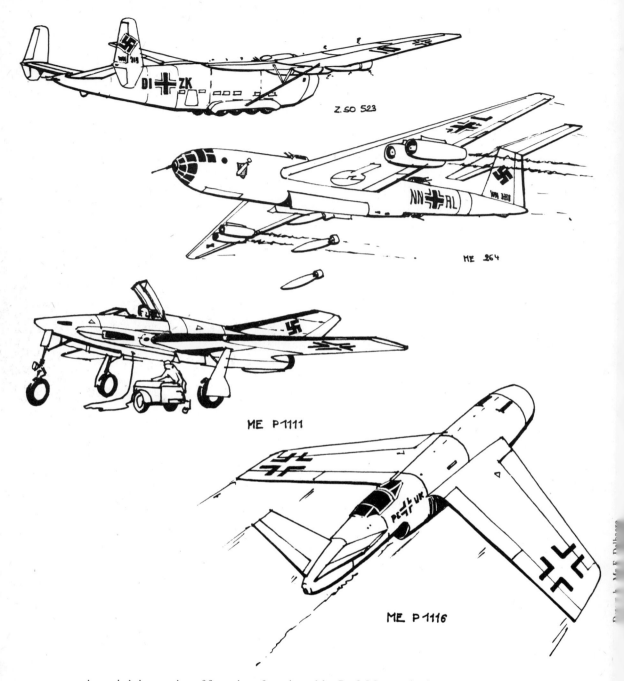

Z.50 523

ME 264

ME P 1111

ME P 1116

An artist's impression of four aircraft projected by Prof. Messerschmitt.
ZSO 523: A development of the Me 323, developed by Luftschiffbau Zeppelin GmbH,
and SNCASO, a French company working under force for the Germans. The Allied invasion
of France stopped all further work on this project. Me 264: A development of the 'Amerika-
Bomber', equipped with four jets. If the war had lasted longer, who knows whether these aircraft
might not have appeared above New York, one day in 1946? . . . while over Germany, Allied
bombers were met by tailless Me P 1111 fighters powered by a Heinkel HeS 011 jet? . . . or by
this strange Me P 1116 V-tailed fighter, proposed by Messerschmitt in 1944?

hands of French-Moroccan troops who passed their finding over to the Americans with great reluctance, and in fact succeeded in holding on to some of them.

In the Messerschmitt factories, work stopped. The concern that at one time employed more than 81,000 people ground to a halt. At Oberammergau, the various futuristic projects were abandoned, never to be realized.

In woods and underground tunnels, American GIs found hidden factories and design bureaux of whose existence their Intelligence had never known. On the airfields, they found hundreds of Luftwaffe aircraft, grounded for several weeks through lack of fuel.

Professor Messerschmitt was forced to leave his beautiful villa looking out on the hills and vales at Oberammergau, and was taken prisoner by the British. The USA, Britain and France asked him to work for them in an advisory capacity, but he accepted none of their proposals. From England he returned to Oberammergau where he was once more arrested, this time by US troops. After his captivity he lived for some time in a shack on a small hill, an out-of-work aircraft designer in a collapsed Germany, his factories which had once hummed with activity a shambles.

Photo: US Air Force

On the way back. Prof. Messerschmitt being received at the Pentagon on 14th October 1953, by the Secretary of the Air Force, Harold Talbott, and the Air Force Chief of Staff, General Nathan Twining. Messerschmitt was in Washington to attend the International Air Pioneer's Dinner, sponsored by the National Aeronautical Association. From left to right: veteran designer, Grover Loening; Prof. Messerschmitt; Gen. Twining; Britain's pioneer designer, A. V. Roe; Harold Talbott; and John McCurdy

And yet, the time would come when he would once more take his place amongst the most outstanding aircraft designers, but that is quite another story.

Appendices

I The Messerschmitt AG in figures

As per 31 Dec.	Fixed Assets	Total Balance in RM 1,000	Total Turnover in RM 1,000	Total Turnover for Export	Number of Employees
1933	620	1,505	166	——	524
1934	1,520	6,711	2,616	——	1,414
1935	3,167	14,182	8,224	——	2,403
1936	6,847	32,044	12,099	121	5,182
1937	12,262	56,668	27,550	909	5,439
1938	10,156	68,078	41,876	1,675	6,491
1939	10,821	109,657	84,518	18,595	8,797
1940	12,053	143,880	101,964	17,584	9,809
1941	13,140	225,565	147,500	14,600	11,591
1942	14,800	323,103	102,000	30,600	11,545
1943	15,293	349,908	255,830	65,478	16,298
1944	29,248	——	250,000	——	21,171
31 March 1945	——	——	——	——	27,263

II Production of Messerschmitt aircraft 1939–45

Type	Number built
Fighters:	
Bf 109	33,675
Bf 110	3,028
Me 210	348
Me 410	900
Nightfighters:	
Bf 110	2,240
Reconnaissance:	
Bf 109	1,325
Bf 110	494

Me 210	4
Me 410	113
Gliders:	
Me 321	200
Transport aircraft:	
Me 323	201
Twin jets:	
Me 262	1,294
Rocket fighters:	
Me 163	364
Total	44,186

III Exports of Messerschmitt aircraft 1939–44

Country	He 45*	Bf 108	Bf 109D	Bf 109E	Bf 109G	Bf 110C	Me 210A–I	Total
Bulgaria	—	6	—	19	145	—	—	170
Finland	—	—	—	—	70	—	—	70
Hungary	—	—	3	40	59	—	—	102
Italy	—	—	—	—	—	3	—	3
Japan	—	—	—	2	2	—	4	8
Romania	—	9	—	69	70	—	—	148
Slovakia	10	—	—	16	15	—	—	41
Spain	—	—	—	—	15	—	—	15
Switzerland	—	13	10	80	—	—	—	103
USSR	—	2	—	5	—	5	—	12
Yugoslavia	—	12	—	73	—	—	—	85
Total	10	42	13	304	376	8	4	757

* licence-built by Messerschmitt

IV Messerschmitt aircraft still extant

(Spanish and Czechoslovakian developments of the Bf 109 and French developments
of the Bf 108 are not included.)

M17	D-779	Messerschmitt-Bölkow-Blohm GmbH, Augsburg, Germany
Bf 108	OY-AIH	Sonderborg Airfield, Denmark

Bf 108	A-208	Messerschmitt-Bölkow-Blohm GmbH, Augsburg, Germany
,, ,,	D-EHAF	Sieberg Airfield, Germany
,, ,,	A-209	Swiss Air Force Museum, Dübendorf, Switzerland
,, ,,	HB-ESM	Ascona Airfield, Switzerland
,, ,,	NX2231	Confederate Air Force, Hobbs Airfield, USA
Bf 109	E	Air Britain, Hurn Airport, England
,, ,,	E DB+3F	Wrecked, Northern Finland
,, ,,	E	National War Museum, Johannesburg, South Africa
,, ,,	E-1	Deutsches Museum, Munich, Germany
,, ,,	E-3	J-355 Swiss Transport Museum, Lucerne, Switzerland
,, ,,	E-4	RAF St. Athan, England
,, ,,	F	National War Museum, Johannesburg, South Africa
,, ,,	F	Doug Champin, Olka City, USA
,, ,,	G	Marshall Airways Collection, Bankstown Airfield, Australia
,, ,,	G-2	RAF Lyneham, England
,, ,,	G-2	Surcin Airport, Yugoslavia
,, ,,	G-6	MT 452 Utti Air Force Base, Finland
,, ,,	G-6	MT 507 Utti Air Force Base, Finland
,, ,,	G-6	National Air and Space Museum, Washington, D.C., USA
,, ,,	G-10/U4	Planes of Fame Museum, Buena Park, Cal., USA
,, ,,	K	John W. Caler, Sun Valley, Cal., USA
Me 209	V-1	D-INJR Polish National Air Museum, Krakow, Poland
Me 410	A-1/U2	RAF Cosford, England
,, ,,	A-3	National Air and Space Museum, Washington D.C., USA
Me 163	B	Deutsches Museum, Munich, Germany
,, ,,	B	Institute of Technology, Cranfield, England
,, ,,	B	Rocket Propulsion Establishment, Westcott, England
,, ,,	B	RAF Colerne, England
,, ,,	B	National Aeronautical Collection of Canada, Rockliffe, Canada
,, ,,	B	ditto
,, ,,	B-1	Imperial War Museum, London, England
,, ,,	B-1	Science Museum, London, England
,, ,,	B-1	RAAF Museum, Point Cook, Australia
,, ,,	B-1a	National Air and Space Museum, Washington D.C., USA

Mitsubishi Shushui (Japanese Me 163) Planes of Fame Museum, Buena Park,
Cal., USA

Me 262	A-1	RAF Finningly, England
,, ,,	A-1a	National Air and Space Museum, Washington D.C., USA
,, ,,	A-1a	USAF Museum, Dayton, Ohio, USA
,, ,,	A-1a/U3	Planes of Fame Museum, Buena Park, Cal., USA
,, ,,	A-1b	Deutsches Museum, Munich, Germany
,, ,,	A-2	RAAF Museum, Point Cook, Australia
,, ,,	B-1a/U1	National War Museum, Johannesburg, South Africa
,, ,,	B-1a/U1	NAS Willow Grove, Penn, USA

Avia S 29 (Czeck Me 262) Military Museum, Kbely, Prague, Czechoslovakia
Nord 1002 (French-built Bf 108) G-AVJS   St Just Airfield, England

| ,, ,, | G-ASTG | Elstree Airfield, England |
| ,, ,, | G-ATBG | Sutton Bridge Airfield, England |

Nord 1002	F-BCAZ	Nabern-Teck, Germany
,, ,,	F-BAUZ	Fayence Airfield, France
,, ,,	F-BFUY	La Pagne Airfield, France
,, ,,	F-BDYT	St Cyr Airfield, France
,, ,,	F-BEOY	ditto
,, ,,	F-BFOJ	ditto
,, ,,	F-BNDS	ditto
,, ,,	N 44	Millau Larzac Airfield, France
,, ,,	N108U	Stamford Airport, Connecticut, USA
,, ,,		Lucht-en Ruimtevaart museum (Air and Space Museum), Brussels, Belgium

V Comparison chart of forest dispersal 'Gauting' vs underground works 'Kematen'

		Gauting	*Kematen*
Productive Area	Planned	6,000	4,500
	Actual	6,000	2,700
Unproductive Area	Planned	10,000	4,160
	Actual	10,000	—
Construction Time	Planned	2 months	10 months
	Actual	2 months	8 months (unfinished)
Construction Workers		400 workers	400 workers
Relation between hours of work per square metre		10 hours	100 hours
Total Cost of Plant		700,000 RM	4,076,000 RM
Productive Labour Force		1,200 workers	729 workers
Lost Time through Air Raids		50 hours per month	—

VI Me 262 Production chart of Messerschmitt AG, Augsburg

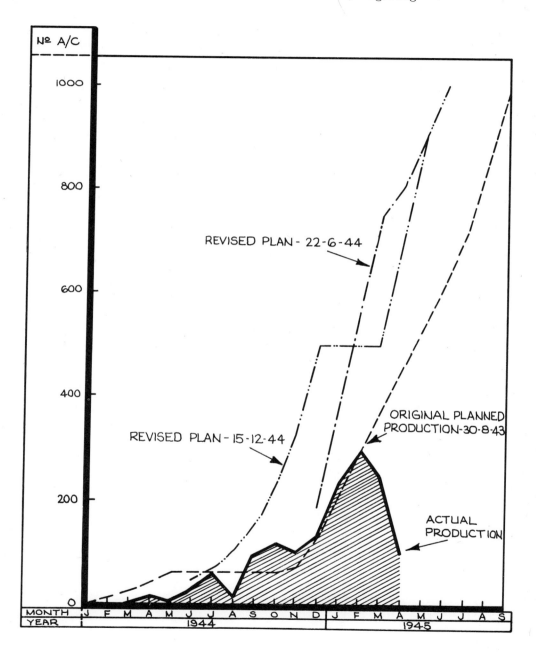

VII Major locations in Germany (then including Austria) where
Messerschmitt aircraft or parts were built, assembled or test-flown

Augsburg
Babelsberg
Brunswick: Neupenertor
    ,,   Waggum
    ,,   Wilhelmtor
Delitzsch
Friedrichshafen
Fürth
Giebelstadt
Gotha
Kahla
Kassel-Waldau
Lechfeld

Leipheim
Leipzig-Mockau
Neuaubing
Oberpfaffenhofen
Ochersleben
Pretzsch
Regensburg: Obertraubling
    ,,   Prüfening
Schwäbisch-Hall
Ulm: Neu-Offingen
Wiener-Neustadt
Wenzendorf

Index